EFFECTIVE COMPREHENSION

A modern approach to comprehend the unseen passages

by

H. S. BHATIA

This book belongs to

____

____

the Bookmaster

D. S. Publishers (India)

Published by :

the Bookmaster

Educational books

DS Publishers India
4325/3, Ansari Road, Darya Ganj
New Delhi 110 002
Tel. : +91 (11) 6525 3158, 3290 1695
E-mail : ds_bookmaster@yahoo.co.in

First Published in 2000
15th Reprint 2018

9788187131458

Typeset by :
Media Arts, New Delhi

Cover Designed by :
Media Arts

Printed at :
Balaji Offset

Price : Rs. 150

PREFACE

Comprehension exercises are conspicuous by their presence in every important examination. Therefore, in this age of effective communication and razor sharp competition there is a need for mastering the art of comprehending unseen passages and being able to complete the exercises with speed and accuracy.

Effective Comprehension will prove to be an able companion. Each unit is divided into the following exercises:

- **Pre-reading exercises**
- **Understanding exercises**
- **Comprehension exercises**
- **Enrichment exercises**

The passages are graded from simple to more complex. As your progress through the book you will be able to pick up the skills required to handle comprehension exercises.

Wishing you all the success

Author

CONTENTS

Unit 1

A Village Fair

I PRE-READING EXERCISE

At a fair we meet people wearing different dresses and outfits. These dresses often proclaim a person's age, sex, country, state, nationality, likings and dislikings (as in the choice of colours, etc.), habits (as of being tidy or dirty, etc.), social, and economic status and sometimes even religion and/or caste. Circle the word in each set below which is not a part of dress.

1. slab	:	turban	:	hat
2. cap	:	shelf	:	muffler
3. damask	:	grill	:	drill
4. scarf	:	steeple	:	waist coat
5. rosary	:	locket	:	niche
6. auk	:	cloak	:	vest
7. chaplet	:	wreath	:	granary
8. bloomers	:	bloodline	:	coolant
9. chandler	:	chap	:	cassock

II READING COMPREHENSION

Read the passage carefully.

I live in a big city which is densely populated and is one of the most polluted cities in India. But I am lucky in one respect and that is that one of my uncles lives at a village which is not far away from my city. So, I often go to meet my uncle, aunt and cousins there.

One day I went to the village 'Sunder Kalan' to meet my uncle and other members of his family. In the evening they took me to a fair that was being held in the middle of the village.There was a big ground where different kinds of stalls and camps were set up by the villagers of that area to sell different kinds of items like eatables, garments, toys, and items related to the beauty culture of women like nail polish, lipsticks, etc.

The ground was crowded with the people of both sexes of different ages. They were wearing colourful clothes. Many of them were eating samosas, jalebies, burfi, etc. Many of them were standing merrily near a juggler, who was showing his tricks. A few of them, particularly the children, were buying toys and were also swaying on swings, merry-go-rounds, and roundabouts. Many children were playing with balloons and a few were watching a magician who was showing his tricks with the playing cards. A number of people were showing their hands to a fortune-teller who was, after reading the lines of their hands, describing the coming of good or bad times in their lives.

A number of stalls had been set up to sell audio-cassettes that had been released by different companies. A few children were dancing to the tune of different songs, running on the decks around. In a few stalls religious audio-cassettes were running and a great crowd of old people was listening to them with great devotion.

In one corner of the ground, two wrestlers were wrestling and the crowd there was bucking them up by making a noise and a few young boys whistled at the sight of some of good shots made by either of them. A referee was also appointed there to keep count of shots.

Both men and women were wearing turbans of different colours. From the dresses it appeared that the people from different regions and of different religions had gathered there to celebrate that festive fair.

Some religious minded old ladies were buying clay images of gods and goddesses, or attractive pictures of deities. Many of them were also buying the cassettes of devotional hymns and religious shabads.

In one corner of the ground a juggler was showing his tricks with his monkeys, and bears. A great crowd was watching and laughing loudly. Many of the men and particularly the children were clapping at intervals of time. At times they were convulsed with fits of laughter.

A few vendors were sitting on the ground. A number of clean sheets were spread before them which were covered with bangles, glass beads, necklaces, bracelets, etc. A number of young girls were purchasing the items of their choice.

In another corner, a snake charmer was playing on his pipe in front of a cobra that had its hood raised. It seemed to be looking continuously towards the pipe. After some time both the juggler and the cobra-man appealed to the people for money. The people paid the money according to their capacity or will. The children clapped and moved away.

On the whole, the scene at the fair impressed me much and I think I will never forget it. Fairs promote interaction among people and also provide them the much-wanted entertainment.

Exercise 1

Understanding the Passage

In each set of the following sentences pick the correct answer (a), or (b) and write it in the space provided for.

1. (a) I live in a big densely populated city.
   (b) I live at a small village. ( )

2. (a) The people were wearing dull clothes.
   (b) The people were wearing colourful clothes. ( )

3. (a) A magician was showing his tricks with sticks.
   (b) A magician was showing his tricks with the playing cards. ( )

4. (a) Some old ladies were buying the idols of gods and goddesses.
   (b) Some young boys were buying the idols of gods and goddesses. ( )

5. (a) In one corner of the ground there was about the between two boxers.
   (b) In one corner of the ground two wrestlers were wrestling. ( )

6. (a) Young girls were spending their money on artificial jewellery and cosmetics.
   (b) Young girls were spending their money on gorgeous clothes. ( )

7. (a) It was the scene of a village fair.
   (b) It was the scene of the day before the Diwali.(   )

Exercise 2

Comprehension

A. ***Answer the following questions.***

1. What is the major problem one has to suffer in big cities?

____

____

2. What kinds of things are there in a village fair which are liked by the young women?

____

____

3. In what aspects does a big city differ from a village?

____

____

4. What kinds of people can be seen in an indian village fair?

____

____

5. How does the crowd behave on seeing a juggler's tricks?

____

____

6. What are the main benefits of fairs in India?

____

____

B. ***Complete the following sentences.***

1. Those people who ever get a chance to visit a village are lucky because ______________________________.

2. The old people were listening to the religious ________ ________________with________________ in the fair.

3. The children were:

   (i) buying ______________________________

   (ii) playing with ___________________________

   (iii)watching ____________________________

   (iv)dancing to ___________________________

4. The young ladies mostly buy __________________ _______________________________ in a fair.

5. Fairs are necessary to ________________________

<u>Exercise 3</u>

Enrichment

Write down the textual words or phrases for the meanings given below.

1. established : _______________
2. food stuff : _______________
3. encouraging : _______________
4. doubled up with laughter : _______________
5. of one's taste : _______________

Unit 2

Rural Upliftment in India

I PRE-READING EXERCISE

The village people are often superstitious. They believe in ghosts and witches. Sometimes, one may be inclined to believe that they are still living in some ancient or medieval period of history. Now match the columns to bring out the correct meaning of each word.

1.	witch	(a)	an imaginary or mythical being of human form but superhuman
2.	wizard	(b)	a nebulous image of a dead person
3.	ghost	(c)	a winged angel
4.	amazon	(d)	a man thought to be having magical power
5.	ogre	(e)	an angel associated with light
6.	giant	(f)	a woman thought to have evil magic powers
7.	cherub	(g)	a kind of female warriors believed by ancient Greeks
8.	seraph	(h)	a devil
9.	dryad	(i)	a man eating giant
10.	demon	(j)	a tree nymph

II READING COMPREHENSION

Read the passage carefully.

Eighty percent of the Indian population lives in villages. There are more than six lakh villages in India. The condition of these people is still a miserable lot.

Villages particularly in the poor states like Bihar, Orissa, etc. are nothing but a hell on earth. We can see their kutcha roads, which go muddy and slippery even with a little shower of rain. There is no proper drainage system in the villages.

Many people in villages live in small houses made of mud. Their houses have one or two rooms, which leak, whenever there is rain. There is a shed for cattle in almost every house. There is no proper arrangement for the storage of dung of these cattle although biogas plants can be installed to get fuel free of cost. But such arrangements can be seen in the villages of a few rich states like the Punjab and Harayana only and those also not on such a large scale as they could be.

In villages the people are mostly dependent on agriculture, poultry and the selling of milk of their cattle. Most of the village people are illiterate. They are superstitious, backward, and poor. They believe in witches, wizards, ghosts, etc. Many of them consume a lot of alcohol, tobacco and also narcotics. Being not very cautious about their health, they never go to the doctors or hospitals to get themselves or the members of their families thoroughly checked up. Hence many of them die even of the fully curable diseases like T.B., cholera, dehydration, etc.

Villages being filled with animal dung and heaps of garbage, are often the breeding places for mosquitoes and flies which spread different kinds of diseases. There is no proper arrangement for pure drinking water or medical aid in many villages. In many of them there are no schools.

There is no electricity in most of the villages. So, the people are still unable to enjoy the T.V. serials. There is no proper system of communication in most of the villages. There is no telephone and even no postal system in some villages.The roads in these villages are kutcha and are not linked with the main roads or highways.

The youths of our country should come forward to work in villages. Small industrial units to generate employment and goods of common use should be started in rural areas.

Particularly such industries as can get sustenance from the produce of the area should be set up in villages.

Most of the villagers are born in debt. They live in debt and die in debt. They have to go for credit to get fertilizers, seeds, pesticides, etc. for their fields. They also depend upon money on credit to get their young ones married.

In every village a pond is a common sight, where the rain water collects and proves a breeding place for germs. In many villages there is no proper system of drinking water. Wells have been dug in some villages, but they are often uncovered and dust particles get mingled with water and make it dusty. But in a few rich villages as in Punjab, hand pumps have been installed and tubewells are also running to cater to the need for water for drinking and irrigational purpose.

Village upliftment is possible only if there are sufficient funds with the government. No doubt the government has taken some steps to overcome these difficulties. Co-operative credit societies have been started. Some special rights have been given to the Panchayats to improve the condition of villages. Subsidies have been given to rural population in many fields. Support prices for agricultural produce have been fixed. In Punjab free water and electricity have been allowed to farmers. More recently certain subsidies have been reduced or abolished. The raise in the prices of diesel, kerosene oil and fertilizers may hit the rural people.

Exercise 1

Understanding the passage

Read the passage again. Put a tick mark (✓) against the true statement and cross mark (×) against the false statement.

1. Sixty percent of the Indian population lives in villages. ( )
2. There is no proper drainage system in the villages. ( )
3. In villages the people usually depend upon poultry, agriculture and selling of milk of their cattle. ( )
4. Most of the villagers have learned the art of safeguarding themselves against many diseases like T.B., Cholera, etc. ( )
5. Villages are often breeding places for mosquitoes and flies. ( )
6. The Indian Government has managed to provide free electricity to all the villagers. ( )

7. Villagers are usually not rich people. ( )
8. Village upliftment needs a great amount of money with the government. ( )
9. Our government has done nothing to put the villagers out of the hell they are living in. ( )
10. The raise in the petroleum products is likely to hit the rural people. ( )

Exercise 2

Comprehension

A. ***Answer the following questions.***

1. Describe the condition of the houses in the villages.

____

____

2. What are the main sources of income of the people living in villages?

____

____

3. Why mosquitoes and flies like to live in villages?

____

____

4. Write two sentences about the development of the communication system in villages.

____

____

5. In what respect do the villages of some rich states differ from the villages of the poor states?

____

____

6. Write at least three sentences regarding the efforts made by the government for the upliftment of the villages.

____

____

____

B. ***Complete the sentences.***

1. Most of the village people are illiterate. They believe in ______________________________ etc.

2. The villages are often the breeding place for mosquitoes and flies because they are filled with ______________ ______________________________________.

3. The roads of many villages are still kutcha and they are not ______________________________ highways.

4. Most of villagers are addicted to ______________ ______________________________, etc.

5. By collecting cattle dung ______________________ can be installed and fuel for cooking can be obtained at a very low cost.

6. Most of the villagers live in debt because they have to go for credit to get ______________________

for their fields.

7. In some villages wells have been dug but they are often _______________________________________.

8. Village upliftment is possible only when_______________ _______________________________________.
a substantial amount of money with it.

9. ______________________________ with water and make it dusty if the wells are uncovered.

10. Some special ______________________________ to the Panchayats to improve the condition of the villages.

<u>**Exercise 3**</u>

Enrichment

Write down the textual words or phrases for the meaning given below.

1. required amount : ____________________
2. uneducated : ____________________
3. a person having excessively credulous belief in the supernatural beings : ____________________
4. a disease which can be overcome by some medical efforts : ____________________
5. produce : ____________________

Unit 3

The Birthday Party

I PRE-READING EXERCISE

Often common nouns form collective nouns in their combined state. These collective nouns look quite different in shape from the common nouns which combine to form them. They offer an important study in themselves. Match the columns 'A' and 'B' to identify each collective noun in column 'A' as per its meaning in column 'B'.

Column A		Column B
1. nosegay	(a)	a collection of ships
2. swarm	(b)	a collection of violent crowd
3. army	(c)	a collection of cattle
4. fleet	(d)	a bunch of sweet-scented flowers
5. mob	(e)	a collection of mosquitoes
6. herd	(f)	a collection of geese
7. gaggle	(g)	a collection of stars
8. dune	(h)	a collection of soldiers
9. galaxy	(i)	a collection of sand

II READING COMPREHENSION

Read the passage carefully.

One Sunday evening I was celebrating my birthday with great pomp and show at my house.

My friends from different corners of the town had gathered there. Most of them were my classmates. We were giving twists and jerks to our bodies with the tunes of Jacky-Macky Band.

The hall was decorated with colourful balloons and bunting. New arm-chairs and small rounded mahogany tables had been arranged in a large semi-circle. The marble floor of the hall began to shine when the lights in the hall were switched on.

We were watching blushing walls as the rays of light from different angles struck (against) them. The ceiling of the hall looked as if it had been ablaze due to two special rows of lights tucked parallel to each other, facing upwards towards the ceiling. Thus the lights brightened up as a single mass.

There was a good gathering in the party. Everybody had put on new colourful clothes. I too, wore a brand new diaphanous pale gold jacket and a new pair of faded stone wash pants. My black leather shoes were shining as they had been well-waxed and polished.

Late at night, I cut the cake and distributed it among my friends. Besides that they were also given bars of chocolate, gem drops, eclairs, and fizzy cold drinks. Then they were served with luscious food cooked by master chefs.

Now the party was over. All of them moved out of my house. I bade good-bye to them and walked into the room.

I was happy to see the centre table in the hall lavished with gifts. As I counted them, they were sixty in number. Many of them were of great importance. They included a pocket computer, a minicalculator, and a mobile phone. Some other things worth-quoting were a pair of striped jeans and an exotic teddy bear.

There was someone outside, for I heard a knock on the door. When I opened the door, I found a boy of about sixteen with a small packet in his hands. "Courier, sir", the boy said while rubbing his gummy eyes. I received the courier pack and moved into my room.

When I opened it, I could not help laughing. It was a birthday gift from my father who was an immigrant in the U.S.A. It contained a bunch of sweet-scented flowers. Besides, on a snow-white paper my father had given an illustration of love through a cartoon. In my heart of hearts I realized that the gift sent by my father was the most valuable one, as it overwhelmed my heart with love and caused the eruption of sudden emotions which made me burst into tears.

I kissed the nosegay of blush pink culled flowers and put it into my bag as it was the gift from my very very best friend.

Exercise 1

Understanding the passage

Read the passage again. Now put a tick mark (✓) against the true statement and cross mark (×) against the false statement.

1. My birthday fell on Monday. ( )
2. The room was quite elaborately decorated. ( )

3. On the day of my birthday I wore a delicate translucent pale gold jacket and a new pair of wash faded stonepants. ( )

4. There were three special rows of lights tucked parallel to each other, facing upwards towards the ceiling. ( )

5. The gifts, I received, were eighty in number. ( )

6. I found a boy of about sixteen with a small box of sweets in his hands. ( )

7. The boy looked quite a smart and well-groomed one. ( )

8. The pack I received contained a bunch of blush pink scented flowers. ( )

9. It was a gift from my father who was an immigrant in the U.S.A. ( )

10. The courier pack was from my very very best friend and he was none else but my father. ( )

Exercise 2

Comprehension

A. ***Answer the following questions.***

1. Why was there a gathering in the narrator's house on Sunday evening?

____

____

2. How was the room decorated?

____

3. What kind of special dress was the narrator wearing on the day of his birthday?

4. What eatables were distributed among the narrator's friends?

5. What were the gifts important and worth-quoting the narrator received from his friends?

6. What made the narrator sentimental after the end of the party?

7. What two contradictory things did the narrator do on opening and studying the courier pack?

8. Who do you think was the narrator's "very very best friend"?

B. ***Complete the following sentences.***

1. My friends from different corners of the town had ____

   ____.

2. The hall looked beautiful due to ________________

   ________________________.

3. I open the door and found a boy with ____________

   ____.

4. I kissed the fresh bunch of flowers which __________

   ____.

5. I burst into tears because ______________________

   ____.

<u>**Exercise 3**</u>

Enrichment

Write down the textual words or phrases for the meanings given below.

1. shining together at the same time : ________________
2. transparent or translucent (jacket) : ________________
3. delicious : ________________
4. filled or completely covered : ________________
5. bunch of sweet scented flowers : ________________

Unit 4

Will Power

I PRE-READING EXERCISE

Human psyche comprises mainly the power to feel, think, plan and will. Of these components, will power has a dominating role in the expression of an individual's personality. Will power in a person may be strong or weak but it leaves its imprint on several areas of human life and experience. Circle the word in each set which is wrong.

1.	unsurmountable	:	unsubtle	:	untheocentric
2.	undeterminate	:	unsized	:	unskilful
3.	unsisterly	:	unsmoked	:	undependent
4.	undexical	:	unsparing	:	unspeakable
5.	undelicate	:	unstarched	:	unsteady
6.	unsuccessful	:	uncredible	:	unsustainable
7.	unsentimental	:	uncorrect	:	unserious
8.	unshaded	:	unshaken	:	uncubous
9.	unshed	:	unsociable	:	undefinite

II READING COMPREHENSION

Read the passage carefully.

"Where there is a will, there is a way", is an old saying. It is also said, "Necessity is the mother of invention". Both these sayings are parallel to each other. The story of the thirsty crow is too well-known to need to be described here.

In history, we read about great and brave men and women who had their will materialised in the face of the stiffest odds. Sita did not lose heart even in the jail of the most powerful demon king, Ravana who was ultimately over-powered by her husband, Lord Rama. Savitri was able to get back her husband even from the clutches of the God of Death. Rani Laxmibai of Jhansi was the brave daughter of India who fought the mighty British Empire valiantly.

When Napoleon was told that the Alps could be a great obstacle in his expedition, he simply said, "There will be no Alps". All of us know how bravely our freedom fighters fought against the powerful and ruthless British government. A large number of them had to kiss the gallows. Many more had to suffer in British jails. At last the English had to leave India.

Whatever is true of martyrs and heroes in history, is true of young men and women in ordinary life. A student who has made up his mind to pursue a particular profession,works hard for it and finally his efforts are crowned with success. It is only through dint of hard work with the spirit of determination that our young men and women have scaled the lofty summit of success in Information Technology and in other fields and made their presence felt even in foreign lands.

All the great advancement of man through the ages has been because of a strong determination and an iron will. Lord Bacon, the Father of Experimental Science, is said to have lost his life while making an experiment with the amount of cold a human being could endure. Madame Curie discovered radium even if she had to work day and night and suffer from cancer because of radiation.

It is rightly said, "Rome was not built in a day". Man has to work hard for generations. Pakistan presented an almost unsurmountable problem for India in the shape of Kargil Conflict, but the brave, determined Indian jawans proved equal to the task. During all the wars with Pakistan, the Indians rose as one man and defeated the enemy. During the Orissa Cyclone, Gujarat Drought, and then Gujarat Earthquake, these were the common determined people who came over the calamity with the sheer power of will.

In view of all this, we can conclude that we should keep our presence of mind when we are in a fix. We should never lose heart. We should continue working hard and follow our path determinedly and doggedly. Success will have to kiss our feet in the long run.

Finally, we should never forget the story of King Bruce and the Spider. Bruce was the king of Scotland. He lost his kingdom and became desperate. He hid in a ruined castle. There he saw a spider trying to climb up a steep wall. The spider fell down again and again but it did not give up efforts till it got success. King Bruce learnt a lesson from the tiny creature that spider was. He came out of his hiding, gathered his brave soldiers and started fighting the enemy. He defeated the enemy and regained his lost kingdom.

We can learn a lesson from this simple story that we should

never give up efforts till success is achieved.

That is why a poet has said,

"Try, try again.

Till at last you do succeed,

Try, try again!"

Exercise 1

Understanding the passage

Read the passage again. Then put a tick mark (✓) against the true statement and a cross mark (×) against the false statement.

1. Sita did not lose heart even in the jail of the most powerful demon king, Ravana. ( )
2. During all wars with Pakistan, the Indians rose as one man and earned victory each time for their motherland. ( )
3. When Napoleon was told that the Alps could be a great obstacle in his path, he simply said, "We will change our route". ( )
4. Lord Bacon discovered radium even if he had to work day and night. ( )
5. Even if you are in a fix, you must keep your peace of mind. ( )
6. It is only by sheer chance that a man can achieve his ambition in life. ( )
7. The freedom of India is an unforgettable

example of the bravery and de‿rmination of human beings. ( )

8. The story of King Bruce and the spider is full of horrible episodes. ( )

9. Madame Curie was a scientist. ( )

10. King Bruce could manage to regain his kingdom because of having been inspired to see the efforts of a spider. ( )

Exercise 2

Comprehension

A. ***Answer the following questions.***

1. Who was Lord Bacon? How is he said to have died?

____

____

2. Who was Madame Curie? How did she die?

____

____

3. What efforts were made by the Indians to attain freedom?

____

____

____

4. Who was King Bruce? How could he manage to get his kingdom back from his enemies? Write down at least

four sentences.

____

____

____

____

5. What did Napoleon say about the Alps?

____

____

6. What is the key to success in life?

____

____

____

B. ***Complete the following sentences.***

1. Lord Rama fought against Ravana and ____________

   ____ .

2. Rani Laxmibai of Jhansi was the brave daughter of India who ________________________________ .

3. A strong will and determination can bring _________

   ____ .

4. King Bruce saw that ___________________________

   ____ .

5. Indian freedom-fighters fought against ______________

____.

Exercise 3

Enrichment

A. ***Write down the textual words or phrases for the meanings given below.***

1. from the hold of : ______________
2. strong and big : ______________
3. strong will : ______________
4. arrive at the result that : ______________
5. stop : ______________

B. ***Write down Antonyms of the following words.***

1. experienced : ______________
2. continue : ______________
3. determination : ______________
4. freedom : ______________
5. suffer : ______________

Unit 5

A Postman

I PRE-READING EXERCISE

Phrases are commonly used in the English Language e.g. 'day by day'. The following phrases all make use of 'day'. Match the Columns 'A' and 'B' so as to get the correct meaning.

Column A		Column B
1. day by day	(a)	something currently considered to be important
2. day in, day out	(b)	from the very beginning
3. these days	(c)	gradually
4. from day one	(d)	at some time in the future
5. of the day	(e)	at present
6. to the day	(f)	continuously
7. day of reckoning	(g)	exactly
8. some day	(h)	the time when past mistakes must be punished
9. by day	(i)	during day light

II READING COMPREHENSION

Read the passage carefully.

A postman is an important member of society. Without him we cannot keep an easy touch with our friends and relatives. That is why he is awaited so eagerly by one and all.

A postman's duty is one of great responsibility as he has to deliver the dak to the right address. He delivers parcels, letters, money-orders, etc. He has to be very careful in the cases of delivering the registered post and money orders because he may be penalized for a wrong delivery.

He lives from hand to mouth. Drawing only a small salary, he is unable to get his children admitted to a convent or public school. So, often a postman's children read in a government school. Sometime back the Government raised the postmen's pay scales to improve their living standard. But the prices of the essential items are shooting day by day and the poor people like the postmen practically find no relief.

A postman's job is not an easy one. He has to work from morning till evening. In the morning he goes to the Head Post Office, from where he takes the dak and puts it into the basket of his bicycle. Then he comes out on the road and pedals from street to street to deliver the dak. He has to work hard under the odds of heavy rain, biting cold and scorching summer.

Earlier the postman used to wear khakhi uniform, but nowadays they are free to choose the dress of their liking. Being a category IV employee, a postman is unable to buy a petrol or diesel-based vehicle. He is always polite and courteous.

For the public he is a messenger of all kinds. He brings pleasant news of births, marriages, successes, etc. and he also bring the news of woes and mournings and many more. Undoubtedly, he plays a key-role in the functioning of the Postal Department. A sight of him in the street awakens eagerness in every heart.

A postman serving in a village reads out the contents of the letters to those who are illiterate. He also writes letters to the relatives of those who do not know how to write. Thus, he also does some social work. He always keeps smiling and talks with everybody in a soft manner. That is why mostly a postman is respected by a large section of society. Lovingly he is called the 'Dak Babu'.

In the modern era the inventions of Fax Machines, Mobile Phones, etc. have somewhat overshadowed the conspicuity of this nice species. But even then we cannot ignore his services which we hope the government will also keep in mind and take some special steps to improve his lot.

Exercise 1

Understanding the passage

Read the passage again. Then fill in the blanks with the words from the passage. You may have to change the form of words in some sentences.

1. A postman is a person who ________________ to deliver the dak to the right address.
2. A postman lives a ________________ life.
3. He is unable to get his children ________________ to a convent or public school.

4. A postman has to work________________.

5. A postman is always ________________.

6. He brings the news of joy and ________________to us.

7. He is also a social worker because he writes letters for those who are ________________.

8. Undoubtedly he plays a ________________in the functioning of the Postal Department.

9. The sight of a postman in the street ________________ eagerness in every heart.

10. The Government should take special steps to________________his financial condition.

Exercise 2

Comprehension

A. ***Answer the following questions.***

1. How is postman an important member of society?

____

____

2. What precautions should be taken by a postman while delivering the mail?

____

____

3. How is a postman helpful to the illiterate people of the villages?

____

____

4. Why does a postman often come on bicycle to deliver the mail?

____

____

5. Write down a few sentences about the financial condition of a postman.

____

____

6. Describe in two sentences the manners and etiquette of a postman.

____

____

B. *Complete the following sentences.*

1. Without a postman the society will suffer very much because _______________
2. A postman is a deligent worker as _______________ _______________
3. A postman lives in poverty as _______________ _______________
4. A sight of him _______________
5. The villagers have a great love for the postman because _______________

Exercise 3

Enrichment

A. ***Write down the textual words or phrases for the meanings given below.***

1. live at the level of subsistence : ____________
2. a person who brings messages : ____________
3. news of happiness : ____________
4. curiously : ____________
5. increasing or rising : ____________

B. ***Write down Antonyms of the following words.***

1. unable : ____________
2. always : ____________
3. soft : ____________
4. important : ____________
5. essential : ____________

Unit 6

The Coldest Day in Winter

I PRE-READING EXERCISE

The last sentence in the first paragraph of the following Passage contains the phrase 'got up'. The word "get" is used in so many other verbal phrases. Please match the phrases having the word 'get' in column 'A' with their meanings in column 'B'.

	Column A		Column B
1.	get at	(a)	make progress in a specified way
2.	get back at	(b)	be elected
3.	get in	(c)	pass (some examination, etc.)
4.	get on	(d)	travel or spread
5.	get out of	(e)	coax (someone)
6.	get round	(f)	take revenge on (someone)
7.	get through	(g)	pass
8.	get in on	(h)	become involved in
9.	get about	(i)	escape or avoid
10.	get by	(j)	reach

II READING COMPREHENSION

Read the passage carefully.

As I live in the northern region of India, it gets very cold in the month of January. I still remember the day of 19th January, 2001. As I woke up in the morning, I got a jolt of surprise to see that it was 11 a.m. In those days I usually got up before 8 a.m.

My little son was writing alphabet on the translucent windowglasses as the water drops were dribbling down from them. No doubt, it was frost which was melting down.

When I walked out in the courtyard, I found my bones shivering with chilly air and there was fog all around. It was difficult to see clearly even the objects lying at a short distance from me.

After having morning ablutions I sat at the dining table for breakfast. I had two cups hot coffee to get rid of the cold that was making my body shiver. On that day I felt that I was growing old because even having wrapped my body with three sweaters and a fur coat, I was not feeling warm and cosy.

After having breakfast I lay in my bed and a hot blower was switched on to keep the room warm. At around 1 p.m., it started raining outside that I came to know since I heard loud clattering sound outside. I wrapped a muffler around my head as if it had been a turban and I also put on woollen socks and I again sneaked into my bed under a heavy quilt.

At 3 p.m. when I woke up again, I found a bright day outside. I moved quickly in the courtyard. The sun was shining somewhat furiously after the rain.

I sneaked out of my house half-hearted because I was feeling that the people around would laugh at me to see me so tightly laced with woollen clothes. But it satisfied me to see the people even more tightly and heavily laced than me with woollen clothes.

Almost everybody had put his hands in his thigh pockets. Many people were eating ground-nuts. Tea was being served in the shops and at the bus-stand. I saw people in small groups sitting round the fire and thus trying to keep themselves warm.

At night, it was broadcast in a special T.V. meteorological bulletin that the mercury had dipped to 2 °C. It was the coldest day in the history of Delhi.

Exercise 1

Understanding the passage

What does the underlined word/words in each sentence mean? Select the meaning strictly in accordance with the passage given and write down 'a' or 'b' in the braket.

1. I got a jolt of surprise.

   (a)got surprise all of a sudden
   (b)got surprise in abundance ( )

2. A translucent windowglasss.

   (a)an opaque one
   (b)a semi-transparent on ( )

3. I sat at the dining table.

   (a) sat on the floor of the table
   (b) sat on a chair that was drawn near the dining table ( )

4. I lay in my bed.

(a) Somebody helped me go into the bed.
(b) I was lying in the bed. Probably I had myself gone into it. ( )

5. The sun was shining furiously.

(a) shining brightly
(b) shining at a great height ( )

6. I heard a loud clattering sound outside.

(a) a continuous rattling or dull confused sound
(b) a piercing sharp sound ( )

7. The mercury had dipped to 2 °C.

(a) lowered
(b) ruined ( )

Exercise 2

Comprehension

A. ***Answer the following questions.***

1. What was the child doing when the frost was melting down?

____

____

2. What did I feel and see when I went out in the courtyard?

____

____

____

3. What was broadcast in a special meteorological bulletin at night?

____

____

4. What made me feel that I had grown old?

____

____

5. What efforts did I make to get myself cosy and warm?

____

____

6. Describe the safeguards adopted by the common people against the cold weather.

____

____

B. *Complete the following sentences.*

1. The bitter cold outside made me ______________

____.

2. I felt I was growing old because ______________

____.

3. The people were eating ground-nuts and drinking tea to ______________________________________.

4. I made a guess that it was raining outside because

____.

5. At 3 P.M. I walked up quickly in the courtyard and saw the sun ______________________________ .

Exercise 3

Enrichment

A. ***Write down the textual words or phrases for the meanings given below.***

1. opaque : ____________________
2. rolling down : ____________________
3. jerk : ____________________
4. having a feeling of comfort and relaxation : ____________________
5. lying near : ____________________

B. ***Tick (✓)the correct part of speech, the underlined word has been used, in each set.***

1. It gets very cold in the month <u>of</u> January.

   (a) Conjunction (b) Preposition (c) Adverb

2. <u>Many</u> people are eating ground-nuts.

   (a) Adjective (b) Pronoun (c) Adverb

3. At around <u>1</u> p.m. it started raining outside.

   (a) Adjective (b) Adverb (c) Verb

4. At 3 p.m. when I woke up <u>again</u>, I found a bright day outside.

   (a) Adjective (b) Noun (c) Adverb

5. I put on woollen socks.

(a) Verb (b) Adjective (c) Adverb

6. It was the coldest day in the history of Delhi.

(a) Conjunction (b) Verb (c) Pronoun

7. Tea was being served in shops and houses.

(a) Conjunction (b) Verb (c) Pronoun

8. But it satisfied me to see the people even more tightly and heavily laced than me with woollen clothes.

(a) Verb (b) Adjective (c) Adverb

9. I was not feeling warm and cosy.

(a) Noun (b) Adjective (c) Adverb

10. The water drops were dribbling down the windowpane.

(a) Noun (b) Adverb (c) Conjuction

C. ***Write down Antonyms of the following words.***

1. easy : ____________________
2. unwrapped : ____________________
3. transparent : ____________________
4. loosely : ____________________
5. engrily : ____________________

Unit 7

The Importance of Being a Doctor

I PRE-READING EXERCISE

There is a great awareness in the sphere of healthcare these days. As such, everybody is eager to avoid diseases and keep healthy. Circle the word in each set, which is not the name of a disease.

1.	dysentery	:	cholera	:	demise
2.	tsetse	:	tuberculosis	:	leprosy
3.	gout	:	bout	:	artherity
4.	arthralgia	:	neuralgia	:	artillery
5.	arteriosclerosis	:	artichoke	:	arthritis
6.	arriviste	:	thyrotoxicosis	:	hypoglyaemia
7.	hyogynous	:	hypogonadism	:	hypomania
8.	hypocrisy	:	hypothyridism	:	hypoxaemia
9.	hypoxia	:	hypocaust	:	hyperkinesis

II READING COMPREHENSION

Read the passage carefully.

When we are asked to find God on the earth in the shape of a human being, our eyes get fixed at the face of a doctor. A doctor is not just to treat us and keep us physically fit. Besides that he also keeps us mentally fit.

A doctor is a respectable member of society. His first mission is to serve the whole of mankind. The job of a doctor is not an easy one. He has to check the patients even at night. He treats patients suffering from mild to serious problems. The range of diseases is long. So the range of different specialists in order to cure different diseases is also long enough.

For the treatment of vital organs like kidneys, heart, lungs, etc. we have doctors who have done M.D. or D.M. in medicine. They advise us how we can keep our blood pressures at the normal level and how we can avoid the development of some fatal diseases like hypertension, hypotension, diabetes, etc.

For the treatment of female reproductive organs we have doctors who have done M.D. in gynaecology. These doctors tell how to keep a woman fit and healthy during pregnancy and after delivery.

Similarly we have child specialists who treat the problems related to children. They tell us how we can take care of our children in a better way. Then we have surgeons who remove the infected tissues and organs from our body and also remove stones from our urinary track or gallbladder. In the modern era we have surgeons who are experts in performing plastic surgery to give a new shape to any part of our body. The most significant kinds of surgery are the bypass surgery, kidney and other organ transplants.

Then we have skin specialists, bone specialists, eye specialists, etc. So, a doctor is like a messiah to our society. He is the real breath of a country and the heart-throb of patients. With the invention of new medical mechinery, it is perhaps not difficult nowadays to transplant almost any and every organ of the human body except the brain. Doctors not only treat the patients, but they also help our country by making the common people aware about birth-control methods and they also perform tubectomy, vasectomy, etc. to keep the population under control.

However, it is now also found that some doctors indulge in the practice of making money even from the poor sections of our society. Such doctors have thus deviated from their real mission. Let them come on the right track.

<u>Exercise 1</u>

Understanding the passage

Put a tick mark (✓) against the true statement and a cross mark (×) against the false statement.

1. A doctor can be said to be God on the earth. ( )
2. A doctor's main responsibility is to keep us only physically fit. ( )
3. A doctor serves only the upper classes. ( )
4. A doctor who has done M.D. in medicine treats us for the diseases like hypertension, hypotension, diabetes,etc. ( )
5. A gynaecologist tells how to keep a woman fit

and healthy during pregnancy and after delivery. ( )

6. But even now it is quite a difficult task to transplant a kidney. ( )
7. To check the birth-control the methods like tubectomy, vasectomy, etc. are being applied. ( )
8. A surgeon treats the patients suffering from bone diseases. ( )
9. A doctor cannot give any kind of awareness to the common man. ( )
10. A doctor is a respectable member of society. ( )

<u>**Exercise 2**</u>

Comprehension

A. ***Answer the following questions.***

1. Why is a doctor said to be God on the earth? Write down three sentences.

____

____

2. What type of patients does an M.D. medicine treat?

____

____

3. How can a doctor be helpful in the controlling of the birth rate?

____

4. What is the function of a surgeon?

5. How is a gynaecologist helpful to society?

6. What is the main mission of a doctor?

B. ***Complete the following sentences.***

1. A child specialist is a doctor who ________

2. The foremost mission of a doctor is to ________

3. The invention of new medical machinery can give a ________

4. A surgeon is a doctor who ________

5. It is found that many doctors are misusing their profession by ________

Exercise 3

Enrichment

A. ***Write down the textual words or phrases for the meanings given below.***

1. a person who should be regarded : ____________
2. passing through : ____________
3. a person who has done a special study of some subject : ____________
4. the backbone of a country : ____________
5. diverged from : ____________

B. ***Give Antonyms of the following.***

1. false : ____________
2. devil : ____________
3. severe : ____________
4. unavoidable : ____________
5. mild : ____________

Unit 8

The Effects of a Heavy Rain

I PRE-READING EXERCISE

Everybody knows something about the rain for good or bad. Often the children love the clouds and the rain. The human beings, the animals and the plants change their behaviour and activities as it rains. In fact, the whole atmosphere changes. Complete the following crosspuzzle with the words associated with the rain (clues also given below).

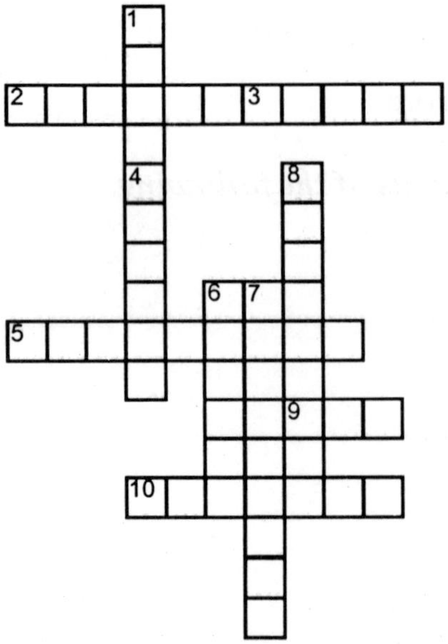

Clues

Across

2. R.........W = that which we see in the sky after the rain
3. W........R = a liquid
5. D........G = fine drops
9. S........N = that which shines in the sky during the day
10. T........R = a loud sound in the sky after the flash of lightning.

Down

1. W.........D = that which blows fast
4. B.........E = that whichblows smoothly
6. C.........D = that which rains
7. L.........G = that which shines serpentinely in the sky
8. D.........S = in which we can't see

II READING COMPREHENSION

Read the passage carefully.

In the early morning of July 6, the sky went crowded with smoky clouds. There was flashing of lightning and gurgling of clouds in a big way. The birds were silent with fear. A cool breeze started blowing. Many old men and ladies brought out umbrellas from their almirahs.

Now it was sure to everybody that there would be a heavy downpour. Everybody was hurrying to reach his destination. Suddenly it started drizzling and the cool breeze stopped. A moment after this it began to rain cats and dogs. It was so forceful that the windowpanes of my room gave a loud clattering sound when the drops of rain struck against them. When I saw outside, I found that there was hailing along with the rain.

In a minute, the drains of our street got over-flooded with the rainy water. Now only the children were there in the street who were expressing their joy by making a great noise and by singing film songs. There was again a great gurgling of clouds and flashing of lightning. The sweet, delightful voice of a peacock that might be at a short distance from my house, fell into my ears.

When the rain stopped, I came out of my house to see the

effect of such a heavy downpour. At first sight on the roof of my own house, I found that the antenna of my T.V. had fallen down. I entered my house and switched on the T.V., but it didn't work. All of a sudden, my eyes stopped at the spot on ceiling from where the drops of rain were falling down. I was surprised at the sight because that was the first time when I found the ceiling of my house leaking.

With a tense mind I again came out of my house. This time I walked upto the fields, which were not far away from my house. There I saw the plants lying down in the fields as the patients lie on the operation tables. The broken stems of small plants looked like the bones of some innocent kids broken by a giant. So many other plants and large trees had been uprooted by the storm.

The telephone and electric wires were badly hit by the rain and wind. Many telephone poles were bent towards one side. The small as well as big ditches were filled with the rain water. The soil had gone slippery. The birds were chirping in the trees and I was sure they must be discussing the effects of such a heavy rain and fast wind. But they were definitely happy.

Exercise 1

Understanding the passage

Put a tick mark (✓) against the true statement and a cross mark (×) against the false statement.

1. The sky went crowded with clouds in the evening. ( )
2. Everybody was hurrying to reach his destination because it was almost sure that there would be a heavy downpour. ( )

3. The windowpanes of my room gave a loud clattering sound due to rain. ( )

4. Our street was clean and no water gathered there. ( )

5. I stepped out of my house only when the rain stopped. ( )

6. I found the ceiling of my house leaking. ( )

7. I went out of my house in a relaxed mood. ( )

8. Many plants and trees were waving as a single mass in the breeze. ( )

9. The birds were chirping in the trees. ( )

10. I saw the plants lying down in the fields as the patients lie on the operation tables. ( )

Exercise 2

Comprehension

A. ***Answer the following questions.***

1. Describe the behaviour of the sky and the birds around you, when it is about to rain.

   ____

   ____

2. Why do the children make a noise in the street during rain?

   ____

   ____

3. Describe the effects of a heavy downpour.

____

____

4. What happens to the windowpanes of the houses when it is hailing outside?

____

____

5. Why were the birds chirping when the rain stopped?

____

____

6. Write down two sentences in favour of rain and two against it.

In favour of rain

____

____

Against rain

____

____

B. ***Complete the following sentences.***

1. In the early morning of July 6th the sky ______________ with______________________________________.
2. There came flashing of lightning and ______________ ____

3. The house became filled with the clattering sound as

____ .

4. Now the children started ______________________

to express __________________________________ .

5. The stems of little plants were broken as __________

____ .

6. The drains of our street ________________________

____ .

7. Many __________________________ brought out

umbrellas from their almirahs.

8. The TV. did not work because ___________________

____ .

9. The small as well as big ditches __________________

____ .

Exercise 3

Enrichment

Write down the textual words or phrases for the meanings given below.

1. mum : ____________________
2. begin to run : ____________________
3. delighted : ____________________
4. entered my ears : ____________________
5. surely : ____________________

Unit 9

Water Management

I PRE-READING EXERCISE

Sometimes, we feel greatly handicapped in life because of our poor English simply because we did not strive enough to learn the basic things in English at earlier stages, such as "the parts of speech". All struggle to learn English at later stages may just prove futile or may not fructify to the desired extent. Hence, it is indispensable to learn fundamentals of English, particularly its grammatical nuances and structures in primary and middle classes. Point out the part of speech of the underlined words.

1. Did you water the rose plant last evening?

   (a) adjective (b) noun (c) verb

2. On seeing the mangoes, the child's mouth began to water.

   (a) adjective (b) infinitive (verb) (c) noun

3. Can you point out the high water mark in the English poetry during the last century?

   (a) adjective (b) noun (c) verb

4. There was water, water everywhere.

   (a) noun (b) verb (c) adjective

5. Mr. Joe was the fool of the first water.

   (a) verb (b) noun (c) adjective

II READING COPREHENSION

Read the passage carefully.

Gujarat experienced the severest drought of the century in 2000. Thereafter reports of water shortage from other states like Rajasthan, Orissa, Andhra Pradesh and Himachal Pradesh have been rampant. A serious water crisis seems to be at hand.

As opined by the experts, irrigated land generally turns saline over a 50 years period. If this criteria is accepted as true, a severe water famine must come into full force even in Punjab during the next two decades, presuming that the Green Revolution started around 1968.

The problem of water shortage is fast spreading. As per reports available, in 1972, a central study put the number of villages with drinking water at 1,50,000. In 1982, it rose to 2,31,000. Now, as the population is growing fast and virtually getting out of control along with the reckless felling down of forest trees, the net outcome of which can be none the better than scarce rain-fall, we have already almost reached a point where fifty percent of our villages have either no source or an undependable source of water for drinking and irrigational purpose.

More than a hundred years ago Malthus put his hypothesis of population outgrowing resources. We ridiculed his theory (thanks to the benevolent monsoon) considering ourselves scientific pundits who could outdo nature and slap the faces of learned, adroit economists, and theorists. Our egoism today dips to the size of a pigmy when the gigantic phantom of Malthus has taken us in its ghoulish clawslike hands only to tear us apart, rich or poor notwithstanding. In the much revulsed but imminent emergence of the demon of water famine, the rich will as much pine and find their limbs wilting and fluttering with hellish pain previously unknown to them and unpredicted by them.

We know universally that there are three main sources of fresh water supply. They are :-

(1) Rain water reservoirs

(2) River and canal water

(3) Sub-surface or ground water

Of these three resources, the first two are controlled or dominated by the government in its own way. The third resource, that is, the sub-surface or ground water is in the hands of the land-owner.

India witnessed the second worst drought of the century in 1987 during the Rajiv Gandhi government. The government then tried to control the third water source, that is, the ground water source, through proposals of banning new private tube-wells and even a harsh legislation on canal water. Irrigation and flood control are state subjects and the states raised a hue and cry against the tough government proposals and the same lapsed.

Now can we secure our future only if we take some drastic measures and that immediately to deal with the imminent water famine.

Exercise 1

Understanding the passage

Put a tick mark (✓) against the true statement and a cross mark (×) against the false statement.

1. The severest drought was experienced by Haryana. ( )
2. The problem of water shortage can never be witnessed by the states like Punjab, Haryana, Himachal Pradesh, etc. ( )
3. There are three main sources of fresh water supply. ( )
4. Sub-surface or ground water is not an important source of freshwater. ( )
5. Malthus put his hypothesis of population outgrowing resources. ( )
6. The shortage of water in many states of India is because of scarce rain-fall. ( )
7. We have already almost reached a point where eighty percent of our villages have either no source or an undependable source of water for drinking and irrigational purposes. ( )
8. The reckless felling down of forests also leads to the scarce rain-fall. ( )
9. In many states tube-wells have been installed to overcome the problem of water shortage. ( )
10. India witnessed the second worst drought of the century in 1987. ( )

11. It is of utmost importance to take some drastic measures to deal with the imminent water famine. ( )

Exercise 2

Comprehension

A. *Answer the following questions.*

1. What is the condition of drinking water in Indian villages?

____

____

2. Why is there danger of water shortage in Punjab?

____

____

3. Why did Rajiv Gandhi government impose a ban on the installation of new tube-wells?

____

____

4. What are the main sources of fresh water?

____

____

5. How was Mathus's hypothesis regarded by the Indians sometime back?

____

____

6. In your opinion, what are the steps that should be taken by our government to manage the water scarcity problem?

____

____

____

B. ***Complete the following sentences.***

1. The state governments were not willing to __________

____.

2. Shortage of water level in India shows a __________

____.

3. The day per day, swollen of population and felling of trees must bring__________________________.

4. We ridiculed Mathus who propounded a theory that

____.

5. Thereafter reports of water shortage from __________

____.

<u>Exercise 3</u>

Enrichment

A. ***Write down the textual words or phrases for the meanings given below.***

1. scarcity : __________________

2. one well-versed in a particular subject : ____________

3. acute : ____________

4. make fun of : ____________

5. self-importance : ____________

B. ***Add '-ed' to the following words after making other changes where necessary.***

1. flutter ____________
2. frolic ____________
3. dribble ____________
4. dip ____________
5. induct ____________
6. dance ____________
7. marinade ____________
8. fret ____________
9. heal ____________
10. talk ____________

Unit 10

Contentment

I PRE-READING EXERCISE

We know that nouns stand for persons, things, etc. But we sometimes do not know or do not try to care whether certain nouns stand for some abstract things which are not solid or concrete. Sometimes, we fail to distinguish between a noun and adjective, particularly when it pertains to some quality, state or activity. So, it is worthwhile to give a thought to this problem.

In each of the following sets, circle the word which is an abstract noun.

1. contentment	:	contented	:	discontented
2. honest	:	dishonesty	:	dishonest
3. happy	:	happily	:	happiness
4. joyful	:	rejoicing	:	joy
5. private	:	privacy	:	privy
6. force	:	forceful	:	forcibly
7. kind	:	kindly	:	kindness
8. restive	:	restlessness	:	restless
9. addict	:	addicted	:	addiction
10. author	:	authority	:	authoritative

II READING COMPREHENSION

Read the passage carefully.

A contented man is a happy man. A man who is always running after money and luxuries of life, cannot get real happiness. As a matter of fact, he is only losing the real happiness which he may otherwise get if he does not pursue these tensive activities.

A man who does not have much money, may be happy if he can get a little with his sincere and honest efforts. With that little which provides him enough for the necessities of life, he can lead a life of contentment, peace of mind, and joy.

A man who has a lot of money, often becomes greedy. A man who has just a few thousand, may be contented with his lot while leading a simple, care-free life. On the other hand, one who has crores or lakhs of rupees wants that his money should multiply quickly and so he is always worried and is under stress for this very reason.

It is most pitiable that a man with a lot of money and property and while himself leading a life of awful luxuries, should forget his friends and even nearest relatives. But a poor man still has the milk of human kindness in him. He is ready to extend his hospitality to his friends and relatives and even strangers who may be in dire need of it.

Contentment is a great virtue which anybody who is clear-hearted and is free from vice can easily pursue. Some people want to lead a contented life, but they are unable to do so. There may be many reasons for it. For example, if a man has vices like drinking, smoking, opium or any other drug-taking, he cannot lead a contented life. It is because he needs constant flow of money to him for his daily uncurtailable needs. If he has no money to pursue his hobbies, he feels restless. He may have to resort to some unfair and undesirable means to get money somehow.

So, in order to lead a contented life, it is of paramount importance that we should be free from all kinds of vices. Otherwise, our dream of leading a life of contentment will never materialize.

Apart from the vices mentioned above, there are certain other vices and habits like gambling, purchasing lottery tickets, extending lavish parties and spending too much on marriages. Many people consider it a matter of pride to spend a lot of money on the marriages of their sons and daughters, even though they may have to be over head and ears in debt. Is it wise on their part?

Certain people, particularly the young people and still particularly, young ladies, spend too much money on their fashionable dresses and cosmetics. They often buy costly foreign-branded cosmetics, attend beauty parlours frequently and arrange or participate in extravagant kitty parties and thereby make their husbands bankrupts. So high-spending is as much the path to loss of contentment as the pursuit of money. It is quite simple. One who spends too much, needs more and more money to spend and for this money, he has to resort to some unfair means and thus he is bound to lose his contentment.

Therefore, the best course for us is to lead a simple, care-free life. We should live within our means. It is not a sin to earn money, but it should be earned through honest means and, moreover, we should be satisfied with whatever we earn. We should keep a strict control on our expenditure. We should not hanker after luxuries which we cannot afford to have. We should always remember: "Contentment is a great virtue". That is why the famous English poet, Alexander Pope said long ago, "Happy the man whose wish and care/ A few paternal acres bound".

Exercise 1

Understanding the passage

Put a tick mark (✓) against the true statement and a cross mark (×) against the false statement.

1. A discontented man is an unhappy man. ( )
2. Money is not the real criteria of a happy life. ( )
3. Contentment is the treasure of an unclear mind. ( )
4. The more we spend, the more we get contented. ( )
5. Young ladies can find contentment if they do not spend much on their fashionable dresses and cosmetics. ( )
6. One is bound to lose one's contentment when one has to use unfair means to earn one's luxuries. ( )
7. One who has crores or lakhs of rupees wants that his money should multiply quickly. So, he is always worried and is under stress for this very reason. ( )
8. One should do nothing to achieve ful=l contentment. ( )
9. Many people consider it a matter of pride to spend a lot of money on the marriages of their sons and daughters. ( )

10. By keeping a strict control over our expenditure, we can get contentment. ( )

Exercise 2

Comprehension

A. ***Answer the following questions.***

1. Write down the qualities of a really happy man.

____

____

2. Write down three lines on "Excessive desire for money".

____

____

____

3. Why drug addict cannot be a contented person?

____

____

4. Why a person who spends more than his income cannot be a contented man?

____

____

5. Write down the secret of gaining contentment even in the modern stressful life.

____

____

6. Can you explain the two lines of Alexander Pope which the author has quoted?

____

____

B. ***Complete the following sentences.***

1. Happiness can be earned _______________________

   ____.

2. A discontented rich person always wants that his money

   ____.

3. A contented person is ready to be hospitable even to

   ____.

4. A drug addict is always in _________________ so, her

   remains____.

5. Certain people take pride in spending on ____________

   ____.

Exercise 3

Enrichment

A. ***Write down the words from the passage for the meanings given below.***

1. satisfied : _______________
2. to have all the time desire for something : _______________
3. chase : _______________

4. evil : ____________________

5. in great need of : ____________________

B. ***Tick (✓) the correct meaning of the underlined word in each set.***

1. Contentment is a great virtue.

   (a) something morally good (b) opportunity

2. It is of paramount importance that we should be free from all kinds of vices.

   (a) great (b) minor

3. Otherwise, our dream of leading a life of contentment will never materialize.

   (a) assume the desired shape (b) become solid

4. A man who does not have much money, may be happy if he can get a little with his sincere and honest efforts.

   (a) hard (b) proceeding from genuine feelings

5. We should not attend lavish parties.

   (a) gorgeous (b) luxurious

6. He needs a constant flow of money.

   (a) occurring continuously (b) a big amount

7. We should not hanker after luxuries.

   (a) have a great desire for (b) worried

Unit 11

Small Scale Industry vs Large Scale Industry

I PRE-READING EXERCISE

In English some expressions such as 'a big change', 'a great change', etc. are commonly used.

Now please tick against the words given below the most appropriate word/s out of the words, 'big', 'serious', 'high', 'strong', and 'great'. Write cross mark against the word not commonly used. The first one has been done for you.

words	big	serious	high	strong	great
1. cost	×	×	✓	×	×
2. crime					
3. mistake					
4. price					
5. speed					
6. accident					
7. care					
8. danger					
9. injury					

II READING COMPREHENSION

Read the passage carefully.

First of all, it is important to understand the difference between the cottage industry and the large-scale industry. Cottage industry, as the term signifies, means industry in a cottage or at home. It means some industrial work done at home by an individual himself or with the help of the members of his family or one or a few workers. The large-scale industry means industrial work in a large mill or factory. The former implies production of some goods on a very small scale and the latter connotes production on a mass or very large scale.

The cottage industry is often a type of rural industry. The small and marginal farmers' work in their fields is often seasonal. Also, it does not keep them occupied the whole day. So, they have ample leisure time. During this spare time, they can manufacture some small items of daily use at home. In this way, they can augment their monthly income and also remain busy throughout the year.

Since the hoary past, India had been a land of cottage industrial units all over the rural areas. As the British came, they made it a point to destroy the cottage industry of India. It is because they wanted to dump their own manufactured items in India. They took raw material from India, changed it into finished goods in their own country and sold their goods in India at very high rates. That is why Gandhiji laid so much stress on Cottage Industry.

Large-scale industry needs heavy machinery for manufacturing purposes. For it, large buildings to be used as mills, have to be built. Apart from manual workers, highly skilled workers are also appointed at various posts. A system of management, administration, manufacturing, processing, testing, research, finishing, sale, etc. has to be set up. The workers have to work like slaves. They have to work according to a fixed schedule. They often have to lead a miserable life in dirty and dingy quarters. They cannot afford a luxurious life as their wages are often very small. The lion's share of the profits is pocketed by the capitalist owners of the concern. Only a few skilled and highly qualified workers may get decent salaries. All others have to lead a miserable and sometimes even a hazardous life.

In small-scale or cottage industry the owner has much independence. He is the master of his own fate. He may work as and when he likes. He gets all the profits of his labour. But sometimes, he may have to face difficulty in selling his produce. Such a difficulty hardly ever has to be faced by a large-scale industrialist. He has efficient and able salesmen (who are well-trained in the art of marketing) at his disposal. They work day and night for him at often a meagre salary.

It may be argued that large-scale industry is exploitative in nature and should be discouraged. No doubt, it can be and often is exploitative. The government and society should take some concrete step to remove this short-coming. Of course, there are certain labour laws concerning workers' working hours, leisure, salary, perks, medical aid, leave, provident fund, gratuity, group insurance, etc. But these laws are so many times violated by the proprietors and the appropriate action is often lacking. Proper remedial measures should be taken by authorities concerned.

In fact, cottage industry and large-scale industry have to go hand in hand. They are and should be complementary to each other. Cottage industry is necessary for large-scale employment and to manufacture small items of daily use like utensils, handloom coarse cloth, bangles, buttons, certain electric goods, pickles, jam, carpets, etc. But large-scale industry is particularly essential for the manufacture of infrastructure and large items like ships, aeroplanes, guns, computers, T.V. sets, refrigerators, steel, fine cloth, sugar, cement, etc. Better tools to make cottage industry more convenient and efficient, can be manufactured in big mills only.

In order to compete at the international level and to fulfil the needs of teeming millions, large-scale industry is essential but cottage industry should also go side by side.

Exercise 1

Understanding the passage

Put a tick mark (✓) against the true statement and a cross mark (×) against the false statement.

1. Cottage industry means industry installed at the outskirts of a town. ( )
2. The British Government tried its best to destroy our cottage industry. ( )
3. Large-scale industry needs light machinery for manufacturing purposes. ( )
4. The workers working in large-scale industrial units usually lead a miserable life. ( )
5. Only a few skilled and highly educated workers may get decent salaries. ( )

6. A large-scale industrialist usually has efficient and able salesmen. ( )

7. In cottage industrial units the items of daily use can be produced. ( )

8. Large-scale industry is necessary to produce T.Vs, cement, steel, etc. ( )

9. The cottage industry should be closed down to put our country on the path of progress. ( )

10. The cottage industry should go side by side the large-scale industry to compete at the international level. ( )

Exercise 2

Comprehension

A. ***Answer the following questions.***

1. Write down the difference between cottage industry and large-scale industry.

___

___

2. Write down the merits of the cottage industry.

___

___

3. Write down the merits of large-scale industry.

___

___

4. Write down the demerits of the cottage industry.

____

____

5. Write down the demerits of the large-scale industry.

____

____

6. How are the cottage and large-scale industries complementary to each other?

____

____

____

____

B. ***Complete the following sentences.***

1. Cottage industry means ___________________________

____ .

2. Large-scale industry means _______________________

____ .

3. A large-scale industry needs _____________________

____ .

4. In a large-scale industrial unit only a few well-skilled workers get handsome salary while the unskilled workers have to lead ___________________________

____ .

5. No doubt large-scale industry is essential but cottage industry ______________________________ .

Exercise 3

Enrichment

Write down the textual words or phrases for the meanings given below.

1. at a massive level	:	______________
2. freedom	:	______________
3. trained	:	______________
4. wages or payment for regular employment	:	______________
5. risky	:	______________

B. ***Tick (✓) the correct meaning of the underlined word/ words in each set.***

1. The large-scale industry is related to the <u>mass</u> production of something.
   (a) of good quality (b) in huge quantity

2. A large number of <u>manual workers</u> are needed in a large-scale industry.
   (a) skilled workers (b) those who can work with their hands

3. They often have to live in dirty and <u>dingy</u> quarters.
   (a) gloomy (b) small

4. They can <u>augment</u> their monthly income and also remain busy throughout the year.
   (a) distribute (b) increase

Unit 12

Science and Religion

I PRE-READING EXERCISE

Since the hoary past, of course, there has been a long-drawn out antagonism between science and religion. Many people still cannot cherish the idea that these two fields both wish good for mankind and their activities and contemplations, though contrary in certain fields, are congruent, overlapping or complementary and supplementary in others. Please circle the words given below which generally or normally cannot be applied to science.

1. experiment	:	spiritualism	:	faith
2. materialism	:	precision	:	exactness
3. superstition	:	conclusion	:	probe
4. contentment	:	inference	:	hypothesis
5. derivation	:	bliss	:	peace
6. ruthlessness	:	beatitude	:	research
7. salvation	:	credulousness	:	reason
8. vision	:	impression	:	formulae
9. truth	:	gospel	:	sermon

II READING COMPREHENSION

Read the passage carefully.

In the past religion ruled supreme over man's life. But later, science emerged on the scene. Slowly but surely, science became a part of man in all walks of life. It developed through observation and experience. Man began to take interest in experiments and thus Experimental or Empirical Science was developed. Gradually it became a part of his nature to make more and more research and probe deeper and deeper into various objects and aspects of nature.

Religion evolved itself from magic and wonder at various phenomena of nature. Man was surprised at the beauty of the sun, the moon, the stars, the oceans, the lakes, the mountains, the dawn, fire, trees, etc. and began to worship these objects. In many cases, he was afraid of what Tennyson has characterized nature "red in tooth and claw" and began to worship several things and objects concerning this aspect, for example, snakes, the sun, the clouds, etc. He also began to worship certain useful objects like the cow, the trees, etc. Later magic became a part of religion. Man began to probe his own inner self and he felt there was a soul in his body. Gradually, he arrived at the conclusion that there was a super-soul which he termed as "God." Emerson uses the word "over-soul" for this super-soul.

Religion having reached a particular stage, demanded unflinching faith. At first the essence of religion was spiritualism. Later, there developed a sort of regimentation. The emergence of different religions, although meant to serve mankind, actually divided it and people of different religions began to fight with each other, giving the name "holy war" to such fights.

Science also developed slowly. But in the modern age, it is taking long strides. There was a time when people believed that the earth was flat and that the sun revolved round the earth. The myth has long been broken. Science believes in concrete truth and not just in assumption.

Religion believes that truth is absolute. But science believes that it is only relative. According to the system of science, today's truth can become an untruth tomorrow. One glaring example is the Newton's laws. These were believed to be absolute and inviolable until Einstein's Theory of Relativity proved them wrong.

There are certainly some common things in science and religion. Both want the welfare of mankind. Only their ways and methods are different. Then both of them claim to have truth as their basis. Religion wants that the truth, it proclaims should be believed in with a blind faith. Science says that it should be studied, probed, tested and only then relied upon. If during research, some new truth or new aspect of truth emerges, science is ready to accept it. But religion is not ready for research, experiment and change in whatever has already been accepted or revealed.

Science has given man innumerable comforts and benefits. It has discovered and invented numerous gadgets, means and methods to make life rich, healthy, cheerful, and long. But it has also invented means of mass destruction which can annihilate all life on earth. Thus science is ruthless in its working.

Religion believes in peace. It has its relationship with inner part of human life. Religion teaches us compassion, mercy, sympathy, love, goodwill, co-operation, courtesy, generosity, sacrifice, renunciation, etc. Science makes us materialistic, selfish, egoistic, flamboyant, cruel and self-centred.

Thus although science is necessary for material advancement and physical comforts, religion is necessary for peace of mind and an ideal and ethical way of life. Religion is, in this way, more the concern of man on individual basis, but the effect of science is widespread and far-reaching. Many people today don't believe in God or religion. But science and religion are not antagonistic to each other. They are both necessary for man for his outer and inner self respectively.

Exercise 1

Understanding the passage

Put a tick mark (✓) against the true statement and a cross mark (×) against the false statement.

1. In the past science ruled supreme over man's life. ( )
2. Man began to worship certain useful objects like the cow and the tree. ( )
3. At first the essence of religion was spiritualism. ( )
4. In ancient times, man believed the earth to be oval. ( )
5. Nothing is common in science and religion. ( )
6. Religion has discovered numerous gadgets, means, and methods to make life rich. ( )
7. Science is necessary for material advancement. ( )
8. Many people today believe in God. ( )

9. Religion and science both are necessary for man for his inner and outer self respectively. ( )

10. Religion teaches us compassion, mercy, sympathy, etc. ( )

Exercise 2

Comprehension

A. ***Answer the following questions.***

1. How is science both the friend and foe of man?

____

____

2. How was religion born?

____

____

3. How did religion divide mankind and what has been its evil effect?

____

____

4. What are the common things in science and religion?

____

____

5. What is the difference in approach between science and religion in the matter of truth?

____

____

____

6. What good can religion do to mankind which science cannot do?

____

____

B. ***Complete the following sentences.***

1. Science believes in concrete truth and not ____________

____ .

2. Science and religion both want the ________________

____ .

3. Science has developed innumerable things providing comforts to man like __________________________ .

4. Religion is necessary for __________________________

____ .

5. Science and religion both are necessary for man because

____ .

<u>**Exercise 3**</u>

Enrichment

A. ***Write down the textual words or phrases for the meanings given below.***

1. result or end : ________________

2. fearful : ____________________

3. slowly : ____________________

4. guess : ____________________

5. many : ____________________

B. ***Tick (✓) the correct part of speech of the underlined word used in each set.***

1. In the past religion ruled <u>supreme</u> over man's life.

   (a) Noun (b) Adjective (c) Adverb

2. Religion evolved itself from magic and wonder at various <u>phenomena</u> of nature.

   (a) Noun (b) Adjective (c) Adverb

3. Science developed <u>slowly</u>.

   (a) Noun (b) Conjunction (c) Adverb

4. Science <u>and</u> religion both want the welfare of mankind.

   (a) Preposition (b) Conjunction (c) Adverb

5. <u>Gradually</u>, man arrived at the conclusion that there was a super-soul which he termed as "God".

   (a) Adjective (b) Verb (c) Adverb

6. Science is ruthless <u>in</u> its working.

   (a) Conjunction (b) Preposition (c) Adverb

7. But religion is not ready for research, experiment and change in <u>whatever</u> has already been accepted.

   (a) Pronoun (b) Determiner (c) Noun

Unit 13

Cinema - its Uses and Abuses

I PRE-READING EXERCISE

Cinema has occupied an important place in our life. It is something which can be said to be multifaceted. As such, it provides us with the living picture of multifarious slices of life. Please fill in the blanks with the words given in the box below.

lodgment	at loggerheads		lounge
special effects	lolly	lothly	loganberry
log-rolling	lay about		like a log

1. ________________ has been a common practice among the authors.
2. The ________________ of green layers on stagnant water is a common sight in the slum areas.
3. The injured pedestrian lay ________________ on the roadside.
4. India and Pakistan have long been ________________ with each other.
5. This movie has become very popular for its superb ________________.
6. Have you ever tasted a ________________?
7. Modern man is always after ________________.

8. Ramu's conduct at the function was ________________.

9. Please don't ________________ at this place.

10. I have nothing to do with that ________________.

II READING COMPREHENSION

Read the passage carefully.

There are many sources of entertainment. Cinema is one of them. It is still a popular medium of entertainment because many people like to see movies on the big screen. The first Indian film 'Harish Chandra' was made in 1913. Ever since the Indian Cinema has progressed by leaps and bounds. Today, India is the second largest producer of films. It has changed the life-style of modern society. Bollywood is very much a way of life in Indian elitist society.

Cinema is a fanciful craze enjoyed by the people of all ages and groups. One can see a never-ending rush at the cinema houses. It is because of its not being a much costly entertainment. The people of every caste and status like to see the movies of their taste. It is a sort of game for children, an entertainment for the freaky young and can be a morally uplifting or morally degrading experience for those who are excessively sensitive or sentimental. As such, films deeply influence our political, social, educational and moral outlook.

Cinema is an important source of conveying certain messages and it can prove a store-house of knowledge if we produce good films, as it leaves a lasting impression on the spectators' minds. It is found that mostly students learn more easily what they are told through films than what they are taught by teachers even through interesting lectures.

Through the cinema documentaries, the government can make people aware of the social problems. Thus a healthy and honest society can be constructed. The news reels provide us the knowledge about the culture of other states and also about the culture of other countries. Through cinema the government can get success at a certain level to remove the problems of population and illiteracy in our country, by giving the public the desired themes, scenes and dialogues. But it does not mean that the government should get full control over film industry.

Film Industry is a big industry. It depends upon so many kinds of skilful as well as unskilled persons. Hence upto some extent it helps the government to remove unemployment. In it many a genius gets a fair chance to bring forth his skill and talent.

Unfortunately, the cinema has its own drawbacks. The presence of excessive amount of violence misguides our youths. Being not much experienced, many youths try to behave like heroes in films. It disturbs their smooth life style when they try to indulge in the dreamy world. In any case, cinema is the breeding place of fashion and glamour.

Many youths are misguided when they watch that the criminals become rich quickly by using unfair means in society.

Cinema can be more successful if we produce good films which convey good messages to the people of every age group. There should not be much violence and crime in a movie. Films should be made with the aim of restructuring a good and gentle society. They should not be made with the aim of just earning money from the youths and labour classes, by showing them violence and sex.

Through cinema we can produce devils as well as gods in our society. Definitely the future of a country depends upon the media including the cinema. Hence our government should try its best to improve the quality of this medium so as to develop a good society, in the coming days.

<u>Exercise 1</u>

Understanding the passage

Put a tick mark (✓) against the true statement and a cross mark (×) against the false statement.

1. Cinema has no impact on the modern man's life style. ( )
2. Cinema is a fanciful craze enjoyed by the people of all ages and groups. ( )
3. Cinema can prove a store-house of knowledge. ( )
4. Film Industry depends upon just a few skilled persons. ( )
5. Many people particularly youths are misguided when they watch that the criminals become rich quickly by using unfair means in society. ( )
6. Cinema has no drawbacks. ( )
7. Through cinema we can produce devils as well as gods in our society. ( )
8. Through cinema the government can make the common people aware of the social problems. ( )
9. Through cinema a healthy society cannot be constructed. ( )

10. Bollywood is very much a way of life in the Indian elitist society. ( )

Exercise 2

Comprehension

A. ***Answer the following questions.***

1. Name a few sources of entertainment widely accepted by the society.

___

___

2. Write down merits and demerits of the cinema.

Merits

___

___

Demerits

___

___

3. How can the cinema be beneficial or helpful in the uplift of the society?

___

___

4. How is the cinema industry helpful in removing unemployment to some extent?

___

____

5. What do you understand by the following lines, "Through Cinema we can produce devils as well as goods in our society".

____

____

____

6. Using your own imagination, explain how cinema can be made to play a much more useful role in society?

____

____

____

B. ***Complete the following sentences.***

1. The cinema is a fanciful craze enjoyed by ____________ ____.
2. It can be morally uplifting or morally degrading for those who____________________________.
3. The news reels provide us the knowledge about ______ ____.
4. As the youths try to imitate the filmy heroes, it distrub ____.
5. The cinema can be more successful if ________________ ____.

Exercise 3

Enrichment

A. ***Write down the textual words or phrases for the meanings given below.***

1. a short-lived interest or enthusiasm : ____________
2. designed : ____________
3. strange or whimsical : ____________
4. amusement : ____________
5. attractive : ____________

B. ***Add the prefix 'un-' or 'mis-' to make the Antonyms of the following words.***

1. fortunately : ____________
2. cast : ____________
3. chance : ____________
4. describe : ____________
5. field : ____________
6. licensed : ____________
7. latch : ____________
8. lawful : ____________
9. just : ____________
10. placed : ____________

Unit 14

The Saddest Day in My Life

I PRE-READING EXERCISE

Life may not be all glamour and lustre. Often it has its dark aspects and periods which overwhelm the feeble but provide cherished opportunities to the redoubtable. Please match the columns 'A' and 'B'.

	Column A		Column B
1.	jugular	a)	consciousness
2.	torso	b)	tears
3.	brain	c)	frankenstein
4.	lightning	d)	sand
5.	crocodile	e)	of the neck
6.	ostrich	f)	day and night
7.	monster	g)	of a son or daughter
8.	road accident	h)	human body without head, arms, and legs
9.	joy and sorrow	i)	alcohol
10.	filial	j)	serpentine

II READING COMPREHENSION

Reading the passage carefully.

Happy as well as sad moments dwell in the same compartment in our life. One can say life is a mixture of joy and sorrow. Some say that they follow each other as day follows the night.

All of us try our best to be happy. But it is a fact that nature does not allow anyone to live in an eternal state of bliss. Such a station may be available only in books or in heaven.

It was the night of August 20, 2001. I put my suit-case into my car and started for Delhi. One of my cousins was with me. He was a young boy of 20.

There was no proper light system on the highway. The night was darker than usual.The clouds were gathering in the sky. The wind dropped. The atmosphere was stuffy. The moon hid behind the clouds and it made the night gloomier.

I was one of those who had a regard for sincere and cautious driving. I still remember that my car was running at a slow speed. Suddenly the tyre of my car burst with a great sound. I applied the brakes.

My cousin and I both came out of the car. My cousin showed signs of worry as he had to sit for the P.M.T. competition in the morning. It was around 1.30 a.m. I applied the jack and loosed the screws to get the tyre changed. After a struggle of about 15 minutes, I replaced the burst tyre of my car with the good one.

Hardly had we run a few metres when a fast running truck from the opposite side, rammed into my car. My car was so badly hit that it rolled like a ball on the road for a few moments.

Then both of us became unconscious. When I regained consciousness, I found myself in a hospital-bed. I asked about my cousin. I felt greatly shocked when I was told that he had lost his life in that horrible road accident.

I am sure, the driver of the truck was dead drunk. That was why his truck rammed into my car after it had taken an abrupt turn. The driver was absconding.

I found that my suit-case was missing. It had some important documents in it and a wad of Rs.10,000/-. I was not very much worried about the loss of money but the death of my cousin made me dumb for a few hours. Even at present, whenever I try to think about the incident, my eyes go wet and my heart goes gloomy. I feel the day was the saddest one in my life.

Exercise 1

Understanding the passage

Put a tick mark (✓) against the true statement and a cross mark (×) against the false statement.

1. Life is a mixture of joy and sorrow. ( )
2. Nature does not allow anyone to live in an eternal state of bliss. ( )
3. The clouds in the sky made the night gloomier. ( )
4. My cousin showed no worry though he had to sit for the P.M.T. competition in the morning. ( )
5. It took 30 minutes to replace the burst tyre of my car with the good one. ( )

6. When I regained consciousness, I found myself in a cathedral. ( )
7. The suit-case contained a wad of Rs.50,000/-. ( )
8. I was not very much worried about the loss of money. ( )
9. The atmosphere was stuffy because the wind had dropped. ( )
10. The car was badly hit by a bus. ( )

Exercise 2

Comprehension

A. ***Answer the following questions.***

1. What kind of atmosphere was there when my cousin and I started for Delhi?

____

____

2. What happened to the car at around 1.30 a.m.?

____

____

3. What shocked the narrator deeply?

____

____

4. Can anybody ever live in an eternal state of bliss?

____

____

5. What was the main cause of the accident?

____

____

6. Describe the author's attitude towards joy and sorrow.

____

____

____

7. Using your own imagination describe the precautionary measures that should be taken while driving on the road.

____

____

____

B. ***Complete the following sentences.***

1. Nature does not allow anyone to ________________
______________________________________ .

2. Mostly accidents on the roads take place due to ______
______________________________________ .

3. To get the tyre changed one has to apply ____________
and loose ________________________________ .

4. The truck rammed into my car after it had taken an abrupt turn because the driver was ________________ .

5. The death of my cousin left me in a state of deep depression and whenever I think about it my eyes go ____________ and my heart goes ____________

Exercise 3

Enrichment

A. ***Write down the textual words or Phrases for the meanings given below.***

1. lacking fresh air : ____________
2. poorly lit, dark or depressed : ____________
3. ran into : ____________
4. unexpectedly : ____________
5. sufficient : ____________

B. ***Tick (✓) the correct expression for the underlined word in each set.***

1. No one can live in an <u>eternal</u> state of bliss.
   (a) lasting (b) ephemeral
2. The wind <u>dropped</u>.
   (a) stopped altogether (b) became weaker
3. A truck <u>rammed</u> into my car.
   (a) brushed past with (b) collided with
4. The atmosphere was <u>stuffy</u>.
   (a) lacking fresh air (b) sticky
5. The driver was <u>absconding</u>.
   (a) had disappeared secretly (b) was unconscious

Unit 15

Culture and Education

I PRE-READING EXERCISE

Education should not be just a parrot like rote of certain facts and figures. It should make an individual rational and contemplative while broadening his mental horizons and outlook. On the outset, it will be significant to ruminate the real and genuine aim of education itself and its generic relationship with culture. So, please choose the words and phrases which you think should be the real aim of education. Tick 'Yes' or 'No' as proper.

	Yes	No
1. To award degrees only	☐	☐
2. To awaken the inner spirit	☐	☐
3. To broaden the outlook	☐	☐
4. To teach how to earn money by hook or by crook	☐	☐
5. To teach to be self-seekers	☐	☐
6. To teach to work for the good of society	☐	☐
7. To teach to follow the customs and traditions blindly	☐	☐
8. To teach to reason out, seek and search	☐	☐
9. To teach to pursue the truth	☐	☐

10. To teach to promote patriotism and universalism ☐ ☐
11. To teach to promote communalism ☐ ☐
12. To teach to be civilized, cultured and ethicial ☐ ☐

II READING COMPREHENSION

Read the passage carefully.

Education does not mean just to get a degree or diploma from a recognized college or university. Education is the tool that destroys the hidden demon of ignorance and gives shape to the new ideas which should be beneficial to the whole of mankind. Thus true education broadens our outlook.

In the modern era man has developed a large number of things and he has got success in bringing so many new ideas in every walk of life. But new ideas, however glamorous, at the cost of morality and honesty, change only into negative factors..

In the modern society one can earn a lot with the so-called new tactics, devices, and gadgets but one should not forget that at every turn of life one has to protect oneself from others who want to merge one's personality and identity in their own through crafty machinations. If you are clever enough to be a shark to others, some others can prove sharks to you.

So one can never claim to be living in a really educated society. Contrarily one can say with authority that one is living in a world of base manipulations and falsehood. In such kind of society, to be successful, it is not necessary that one should be kind or honest but what is the most important thing is to become tactful dishonest and all that untruth brings in its train. But is it commendable for us to be called "educated" while possessing such wiles of the Devil?

It is all happening due to our defective education system. Our education policy is directionless, lacking in definiteness of aims, goals, and objectives, resulting in absence of link between education, development and community participation. Even in your own houses, you can see that your son or daughter, if he or she is going to school or college, would take not more than a minute in answering your question regarding what he or she wants to be in his or her life, but he or she would take a full day or even more time in answering your question "How?". It is because an honest path in the modern world is too vague, if not non-existent.

In many countries the system of education has been given a new touch by introducing a number of technical lessons even at the primary level. Along with that full emphasis is laid on moral education from the very beginning. It is because the educationists of those countries believe that education should provide knowledge, skills, and manners as also values, ethics and culture.

Culture is the main instrument for disseminating the accomplishments of human civilization. Culture has the central role to play in the economic and social life of a nation.

Culture makes a nation perfect by showing it a new direction of morality and honesty to its citizens. It keeps a common man away from the so-called crimial activities and educates him about the real meaning of life and that is to do good to his nation and to the whole world. Does this sort of man need a heap of degrees from an education centre? Rightly did J. Krishnamurthy say that in certain cases even an illiterate man can be considered an educated one in the real sense. He was probably talking of culture consciously or unconsciously. And this is exactly what many of our the socalled "educated" young men are lacking. Do they deserve to be regarded as "educated" ones in the real sense of the word?

Exercise 1

Understanding the passage

Put a tick mark (✓) against the true statement and a cross mark (×) against the false statement.

1. In the modern era man has developed a large number of things and ideas at the cost of morality. ( )
2. Education is the tool that can kill or destroy the hidden demon of ignorance. ( )
3. We are living in a world of honesty and truthfulness. ( )
4. We are getting education to become tactful, which is actually not the real motive of education. ( )
5. Our education system is well developed and it enables us to avail ourselves of more opportunities on the basis of honesty. ( )
6. In many countries full emphasis is laid on moral education from the very beginning. ( )

7. Culture has no role in the economic and social life of a nation. ( )

8. If an uneducated person is aware of his surroundings and culture and has a considerable amount of honesty and truthfulness, he can be said to be an educated one. ( )

9. J. Krishnamurthy was probably talking of culture consciously or unconsciously. ( )

<u>**Exercise 2**</u>

Comprehension

A. ***Answer the following questions.***

1. What is the main benefit of education?

____

____

2. What is the real meaning of 'If you are clever enough to be a shark to others, some others can prove sharks to you'?

____

____

3. In what respect is our education policy defective?

____

____

4. What kind of education at the primary level does the author favour?

____

___

5. What is the role of culture according to the author?

___

___

6. Using your imagination, point out how even an illiterate person be considered educated in certain cases? Write three sentences.

___

___

B. *Complete the following sentences.*

1. The hidden demon of ignorance can be ___ ___.

2. In the modern society ___ ___.

3. A defective education system directly affects the society and makes it ___.

4. Culture makes a nation perfect by ___ ___.

5. In many countries moral education is considered to be of utmost importance because the educationists of those countries think that ___ ___.

Exercise 3

Enrichment

A. ***Write down the textual words or phrases for the meanings given below.***

1.accepted by the government : ____________

2.tricks : ____________

3.stress : ____________

4.illegal activities : ____________

5.achievements : ____________

B. ***Give one word or some other words for the following.***

1. put an end to the existence of something : ____________
2. that which is imperfect : ____________
3. one who is clever or crafty : ____________
4. that which means stress : ____________
5. that which means spreading : ____________
6. achievements : ____________
7. goal : ____________
8. having glamour : ____________
9. without realising : ____________
10. acknowledge the validity of : ____________

Unit 16

Biogas

I PRE-READING EXERCISE

A man, and for that matter a nation, has sometimes to face apparently insurmountable odds in his (or its) life. To point out certain words, mainly adjectives or participles, in their negative forms (to form antonyms), we often use the prefix 'in-'. But sometimes, the word requires some other prefix, etc. instead of 'in-' and the use of 'in' becomes wrong. So please circle the word in each set, which is incorrect.

1.	incorrigible	: incredulous	: inauthorised
2.	incorrupt	: inavailable	: incumbent
3.	incurable	: incurious	: inattributed
4.	inconvertible	: incorporated	: inavoidable
5.	inaware	: inconsequential	: inconsiderable
6.	inbalanced	: incommodious	: included
7.	inburied	: incandescent	: incarnate
8.	incautious	: incendiary	: incaged
9.	incisive	: inblushing	: incipient

II READING COMPREHENSION

Read the passage carefully.

India is a big but densely populated country. So the consumption of needs of daily life here is greater than that in many other countries of the world. But production of many things here is far less than that required. Energy is one of such things. We have power plants, which change water energy into electrical energy. We also have plants which change wind energy into electrical energy. But still we are far behind to fulfil the actual demand.

With the increase in population there is a great rise in the demand for coal, petroleum, and electricity. The per year energy demand of the year 2000 A.D. was estimated to be about 400 million tonnes of coal, 100 million tonnes of petroleum, and 1,00,000 mega watts of electricity. All such huge demands put a big question mark on the economic progress of India.

But there is a way for India to tackle the problem of electricity or energy or fuel upto some extent at local levels, at least and that is the production of biogas.

What is biogas?

Biogas being a mixture of various gases contains 50-60 per cent of Methane, 30-40 per cent of Carbondioxide, 1-5 per cent of Hydrogen, 1 per cent of Nitrogen, 0.1 per cent of Hydrogen Sulphide, 0.1 per cent of Oxygen, and 0.1 per cent of Water Vapour. While having a calorific value of 4713-5735 kcal/m^3 biogas can replace 12.30 kg of cow dung cakes, 3.50 kg of wood, 0.62 litre of kerosene oil, 0.52 litre of diesel, 0.43 kg of LPG (Liquid Petroleum Gas) and 4.70 kilo watt of electricity.

How India can achieve the target.

Experts have calculated that India can achieve the target of production of required amount of fuel. India being an agriculture-based country, has the largest number of animals. So, the dung of these animals can be used in a big way to produce biogas which through pipes or some other means can be supplied from house to house. Through this scheme, our government can not only save the money that it has to spend on LPG or kerosene oil but this method will also be beneficial to control the **pollution** to some extent.

What action should be taken by the government in this regard?

The **state governments** should come out in a big way to help the **poor people** in villages and loans should be given at a lower interest rate. The other method is that the Panchayats should be allowed to install a big biogas plant in each village for which the State Government or Central Government should help it. And the gas for fuel should be supplied to the villagers through pipes at a cost lower than that of LPG. For that a few young-boys can be given employment and the net profit from this process can be shared by the State or Central Government with the Panchayat, while supplying cheaper electricity to the villagers.

Thus, this step can be a promising one.

Exercise 1

Understanding the passage

Put a tick mark (✓) against a true statement and a cross mark (×) against a false statement.

1. Though India is big country yet the consumption of zeverything is quite low here. ( )
2. Production of many things here is far less than that required. ( )
3. With the increase in population there is a great rise in the demand for coal, petroleum products, electricity, etc. ( )
4. Biogas is the answer to fully solve the energy problem. ( )
5. Biogas is a mixture of different gases. ( )
6. By using biogas as a fuel a great amount of foreign currency can be saved that India has to spend to buy fuel for us. ( )
7. Biogas plants in the villages will also be helpful to solve the unemployment problem to some extent. ( )
8. Biogas will pollute the atmosphere. ( )
9. The great problem with biogas plant is that through pipes the fuel cannot be sent from the plant to different houses in a village. ( )
10. The Central Government should urge the people to start biogas plants and it should also help the villagers to set up such plants throughout the country. ( )

Exercise 2

Comprehension

A. *Answer the following questions.*

1. Why is the consumption of everything greater in India?

____

____

2. What is the composition of biogas?

____

____

3. How can biogas plants be helpful to solve the problem of unemployment to some extent?

____

____

4. Name different kinds of sources of energy mentioned in the lesson.

(a) ____________________ (b) ____________________

(c) ____________________ (d) ____________________

(e) ____________________ (f) ____________________

5. How can Central as well as State Governments be helpful in setting up biogas plants in every village across the country?

____

____

____

6. How according to the author can India achieve the target of production of required amount of fuel?

____

____

____

B. ***Complete the following sentences.***

1. The consumption of nearly everything is greater _____ ____________________________________ .
2. Indian economical progress is slow due to the ______ ____________________________________ .
3. Biogas can replace ________________________ .
4. Installation of biogas plants will solve the problems of ____________________________________ .
5. India is a big country. So, the consumption of everything here is greater than________________________ .
6. Biogas is a mixture of ________________________ gases, etc.
7. India can achieve the target of ____________________ .
8. The large number of animals can be a boon to India, because the more is the animal dung, ________________ .
9. Biogas plants can be a ________________________ opportunity for the unemployed.

10. The State Governments should come out in a big way to help ________________________________.

11. With the help of biogas plants, electricity at ____________ ____________________ can be supplied to the villagers.

12. Panchayats should be allowed ____________________.

13. This step can be ______________________________.

Exercise 3

Enrichment

A. ***Write down the textual words or phrases for the meanings given below.***

1. increase : ____________________
2. to solve the problem : ____________________
3. aim : ____________________
4. at a large scale : ____________________
5. give : ____________________

B. ***Give Antonyms of the following.***

1. supply : ____________________
2. waste : ____________________
3. harmful : ____________________
4. destroy : ____________________
5. profit : ____________________

Unit 17

A Good Student

I PRE-READING EXERCISE

It is a well-known saying described to Aristotle that man is a social animal. As such, we still compare many of our activities to those of animals. Among the domestic animals, we are most inclined to consider the claim of the dog to the closest to us. Even otherwise, "Dog" is a commonly used word in English. So, match the columns to express the correct meaning of the phrase concerned.

1. dog and pony show	(a) deteriorate horribly
2. every dog has his day	(b) the havoc accompanying military conflict
3. the dogs of war	(c) an elaborate display
4. go to the dogs	(d) consider someone worthless
5. to rain cats and dogs	(e) a life full of misery
6. throw someone to the dogs	(f) everyone has a moment of good luck
7. a dog's life	(g) used to emphasise how delighted someone is
8. sleep like a dog with two tails	(h) to rain heavily
9. put on the dog	(i) a long time
10. a dog's age	(j) behave in a pretentious way

II READING COMPREHENSION

Read the passage carefully.

A man has to shoulder varied responsibilities in life. For this, he has to be a good student to start with. A student really means not only one who studies the prescribed courses and subjects. It means more than this and that is that he should be aware that he is not only just a student but also the future of his society and country. So, he must be conscious of his responsibilities and duties towards his country and the society at large.

First of all, to be a good student, one should not take part in dirty politics of any sort which can only lead him to ruin and if once he gets caught in the trap of such sort of exercises he would never be able to find an outlet. It is because the crafty politicians and the people of influence will use him like a puppet in their hands. And in the long run, he will be treated as a dog at their door. If you would like to lead this sort of life which is full of disrespect let me say it is okay for you. But one should not forget that many young people in the world lose golden opportunities due to loss of character and self-respect.

The second most important thing for a good student is that he should be sympathetic to other students who belong to the weaker sections of society. A rich student who wants to be a good one, can distribute books, pens, pencils, and other stationery items among the poor students. He can pay their monthly fee and thus help them in continuing their studies. Cash money should not be paid to poor students because it can create a feeling of inferiority among them or tempt them to get addicted to some vices. But still more important thing is to help the poor students in their studies so that they can stand on their own legs in life. Just giving them stationery or money can hurt their self-respect.

A good and active student attends all the functions at school or college. He also takes part in other extra-curricular activities like games, debates, group songs, quiz contests, etc. It is a different matter that he can have one of the games like cricket, hockey, badminton, table tennis or lawn tennis as his most favourite game to which he gives more attention.

A good student never makes fun of his teachers or class-mates. He rather tries his best to make his class-mates understand that a teacher is second only to God. It is because it is only the teacher in the whole society who genuinely desires to see the youths to rise to a level higher than he himself is at and finds happiness in that whereas all others, sometimes even the near relatives feel jealous or envious.

A good student can inspire his friends and they can together go in small groups in the rural areas to make the people aware of national problems like population, illiteracy, poverty, disease etc. So, he can work as a bridge between the government and the villagers and can awaken an important section of society from its deep slumber to make his country economically and socially strong and healthy.

Finally, a good student never neglects his studies. He comes off with flying colours in every examination. Besides his character, he also takes care of his health. He respects his parents as much as his teachers.

Exercise 1

Understanding the passage

Put a tick mark (✓) against the true statement and cross mark (×) against the false statement.

1. None is as faithful as a man is. ( )
2. Everybody should be conscious of his responsibilities and duties towards his country and the society at large. ( )
3. A good student does not take part in dirty politics. ( )
4. The politicians are in the habit of using the common man as a puppet in their hands. ( )
5. Good character is necessary to take advantage of the golden opportunities in life. ( )
6. A good student should not show sympathy to other students who belong to the weaker sections of society. ( )
7. A good student should not give cash money to the poor students because it can create a feeling of inferiority among them. ( )
8. A good student does not take part in extra-curricular activities. ( )
9. A good student does not make fun of his teachers and class-mates. ( )
10. A good student takes care of his health. ( )

Exercise 2

Comprehension

A. *Answer the following questions.*

1. What are the qualities that a good student should have?

 ____

 ____

2. How should a good student help his poor class-mates?

 ____

 ____

3. Why should not a good student give cash money to poor students?

 ____

 ____

4. In what kind of activities a good student does not take part?

 ____

 ____

5. Why should we respect our teachers?

 ____

 ____

6. What can a good student do for the rural people?

 ____

 ____

B. ***Tick the correct meanings for the underlined words in each set.***

1. The crafty politicians use the students like a <u>puppet in their hands</u>.

   (a) according to their own will

   (b) take too much work from them

   (c) treat them in a rude manner

2. It can create a feeling of inferiority among them or tempt them <u>to get addicted to some vices</u>.

   (a) to become terrorists

   (b) to develop some bad habbits

   (c) to do nothing

3. A good student can awaken an important section of society from its <u>deep slumber</u>.

   (a) sleep or indifference

   (b) a life of luxury

   (c) misdeeds

4. A good student <u>comes off with flying colours</u>.

   (a) achieves a grand successs

   (b) wears colourful clothes

   (c) does not copy during the examinations

Exercise 3

Enrichment

A. ***The collection of different things are given different names. Match the Columns, showing different collections and their names (collectively).***

1. a bouquet	(a)	a collection of ships
2. a herd	(b)	a collection of flowers
3. a fleet	(c)	a crowd of cattle
4. a range	(d)	a mass of cotton
5. a swarm	(e)	a collection of hills or mountains
6. a bale	(f)	a collection of files
7. a dune	(g)	a collection of mosquitoes
8. a pile	(h)	a big mass of sand
9. a stack	(i)	a collection of bricks arranged in a proper order

B. ***Use the following idioms and phrases into sentences of your own.***

1. come off : ____________
2. lead to : ____________
3. take part in : ____________
4. aware of : ____________
5. jealous of : ____________

Unit 18

Modern Man and Wild Animals

I PRE-READING EXERCISE

We say 'buzzing of a phone' or 'trimming of a phone'. Both the expressions are correct. Match the following columns containing sounds.

	Column A		Column B
1.	an elephant	(a)	bleats
2.	a hen	(b)	croaks
3.	a goat	(c)	trumpets
4.	a wolf	(d)	hums
5.	a bee	(e)	clucks
6.	a snake	(f)	brays
7.	a mule	(g)	howls
8.	a frog	(h)	hisses
9.	a cat	(i)	buzzes
10.	a fly	(j)	mews

II READING COMPREHENSION

Read the passage carefully.

It is quite possible to make a guess how diligently one has to work to earn one's livelihood. For that we can see our parents working throughout the day.

As my own experience, I would like to mention my father's lifestyle. He gets up early in the morning and keeps a mobile phone in his hands. Then he makes a few calls to his clients. He also makes use of it when he has to confirm something from his subordinates. On many occasions he attends calls from his co-business-men. Hence the day for him starts with the buzzing of the phone and even at night his mobile phone remains under his pillow and gives out a trimming sound every now and then.

On the other hand, the wild life is not only full of struggle but also precipitant danger. I am saying this in an authoritative voice because once I had a chance to look at the lifestyle of wild animals. I alongwith one of my uncles, drove to the olivaceous slope of a hill. It was covered with dense growth of different kinds of plants.

Through my binoculars I saw a lion hunting. As soon as the lion saw a deer, he began to run after it. The deer jumped over the dense growth in the jungle and hid in a thick bush. The lion reached the bush and stopped near it. After a moment, he began to move round the bush.

Definitely, the deer was in trouble. I too was frightened to perceive the fate of the deer. I pulled a handkerchief out of my pocket and dabbed (at) my wet face with it to get it dry.

After sometime the deer came out of the bush thinking that

the lion had gone. But it was a very serious mistake committed by the dear. The lion was already there in wait for it. As soon as the lion saw the deer, he pounced on it and tore it from limb to limb.

<u>Exercise 1</u>

Understanding the Passage

Put a tick mark (✓) against the true statement and a cross mark (×) against the false statement.

1. It is quite possible to earn one's livelihood without doing work diligently. ( )
2. I always see my parents doing nothing. ( )
3. My father gets up early in the morning and keeps a mobile phone in his hands. ( )
4. Even in the morning he makes a few calls to his co-business-men to earn his family's livelihood. ( )
5. Wild life is full of laziness and happiness. ( )
6. The slope of the hill was of dusky yellow colour. ( )
7. The deer ran fast and jumped over the dense growth in the jungle to save its life. ( )
8. When the lion ran away, the deer found itself free from trouble. ( )
9. I got my face wet with sweat due to fear. ( )
10. The lion pounced on the deer and tore it frcm limb to limb. ( )

Exercise 2

Comprehension

A. *Answer the following questions.*

1. Describe the wildlife, strictly in accordance with the passage. Use present tense throughout.

   ______

   ______

   ______

2. How a student can achieve grand success in an examination by working hard?

   ______

   ______

3. Describe the hectic life of a businessman as given in the passage.

   ______

   ______

   ______

4. How did the lion hunt the deer?

   ______

   ______

5. Is the life of an ordinary animal less safe than that of a man? If so why?

   ______

   ______

____

6. Using you own imagination, suggest three measures which should be taken to ensure the security and safety of the common people.

____

____

____

B. ***Complete the following sentences.***

1. My father takes much interest in his business as _____

____ .

2. I know that the wild life is also _______________

____ .

3. I pulled a handkerchief out of my pocket and _______

____ .

4. The lion was already there in _______________ .

5. The lion pounced on it and _______________ .

<u>Exercise 3</u>

Enrichment

A. ***Choose the appropriate words from the passage for the meanings given below.You may change the parts of speech.***

	Meanings		*Textual words*		*Words suggested*
1.	hard working	:	__________	:	__________

2. juniors : ____________ : ____________

3. ringing sound : ____________ : ____________

4. of dusky yellowish green colour : ____________ : ____________

5. tore into pieces : ____________ : ____________

B. ***Nature has provided different colours to the different things.***

Match the following columns containing the names of different colours.

1.	Olivaceous	(a)	blackish
2.	blush	(b)	dusky yellow
3.	nigrescent	(c)	(of complexion) red
4.	luteous	(d)	deep orange yellow
5.	pepper-and-salt	(e)	(of face or complexion) red - a sign of good health
6.	pie-bald	(f)	pink
7.	sanguine	(g)	(of a horse) having white and dark patches
8.	rubicund	(h)	cloth of dark and light wools woventogether

Unit 19

The Happiest Day of My Life

I PRE-READING EXERCISE

The parts of the body denote different meanings when used alongwith other words. Here is the example of "hand" the usage of which is so common that often we are not even conscious of it. We frequently use the word "hand" in our speech and for writing purposes.

Now match the phrases in column 'A' with the meanings in column 'B'.

	Column A		Column B
1.	at hand	(a)	not under control
2.	in hand	(b)	close by
3.	in safe hands	(c)	through the agency of
4.	out of hands	(d)	ready for use if required
5.	set one's hand to	(e)	have as much work as one can do
6.	on every hand	(f)	protected by someone
7.	hands down	(g)	with hands joined
8.	at the hands of	(h)	start work on
9.	hand in hand	(i)	easily and decisively
10.	have one's hands full	(j)	all around

II READING COMPREHENSION

Read the passage carefully.

The feeling of examination "at hand" was already over. It was the day of 31st March, 2001. It was the day when my result was to be published in the newspaper. That day I got up early in the mornng. My attention was concentrated on the result that was about to appear.

It was because my whole life depended on my success in the competition of Computer Engineering Entrance test that I had taken in the month of January, 2001. In those days we were very poor people. The only earning hand in my family was my father.

I wanted to support my family, so as to bring happy moments for my mother, for my little brother and my very loving, small doll like sister. But until that I could not understand what to do to make all this a fact.

The only thing I could understand was that it would make us rich and enable my father to resign his arduous low-class job if I was able to go abroad and make a buck there. And it was possible only if I could learn something that would have an immense value in rich countries.

Then the idea of Computer Engineering struck my mind. I had learnt that the Indian Computer Engineers were having a hey-day abroad.

I was sitting at the table and a cup of tea was served to me. Suddenly I heard a low thud in the courtyard of my house. I was sure that it was the newspaper I was waiting for. I ran for it. When I passed through the result, I could not keep my joy within the boundaries of my heart. I whistled twice with full might and raised my arms towards the sky.

I had passed the examination. The news spread in the whole locality like wild fire. All my neighbours came to congratulate me. And many of them spoke words of great love and inspiration. The members of my family were not able to express their happiness. My mother was so happy that tears of joy erupted out of her eyes and rolled down on her wrinkled cheeks.

In the evening my father entered the house. Before I could tell him about my success, he gave me a moment of extreme surprise and happiness by telling me that he had won a lottery for Rs.1,000,000/-.

That day was an unforgettable one for me. Although I have earned so far millions of dollars, yet I have never found myself as happy as I was on the day of 31st March, 2001.

Exercise 1

Understanding the passage

Put a tick mark (✓) against the true statement and a cross mark (×) against the false statement.

1. My result was published in a newspaper on 31st March, 2001. ( )
2. Much depended upon the result of my Pharmacy Test. ( )
3. In those days my father was the only earning hand in my family. ( )
4. I wished to see every member of my family happy. ( )
5. I wished that my father should stick to his arduous job. ( )

6. The low thud in courtyard, was the sound produced when a cat jumped down on the hard ground. ( )

7. I whistled thrice with full might and raised my arms towards the sky. ( )

8. I had passed the examination. ( )

9. My mother could not keep her joy within the boundaries of her heart and the tears rolled down her wrinkled cheeks. ( )

10. My brother won a lottery worth Rs.1,000,000/-. ( )

Exercise 2

Comprehension

A. ***Answer the following questions.***

1. What made the speaker so eager on the morning of 31st March, 2001?

____

____

2. Why was it indispensable for the speaker to join the Computer Engineering Course?

____

____

3. How did the speaker express his joy?

____

____

4. What happened to the speaker's mother and why?

____

____

5. What good news was given by the speaker's father on the evening of 31st March, 2001?

____

____

6. How many members were there in the family of the speaker

____

____

B. ***Complete the following sentences.***

1. I competed to get admission to the Computer Engineering Course because ____________________
____.

2. The Indian Computer Engineer have earned __________
______________________________________abroad.

3. The news of my success in the examination spread _____
____.

4. The immense amount of happiness that filled my mother's heart was felt by me when I found __________
____.

5. Although I have earned so far millions of dollars __________

____ .

Exercise 3

Enrichment

A. ***Write down the textual words or phrases for the meanings given below.***

1. a tough job : ____________
2. great value : ____________
3. all of a sudden : ____________
4 with full strength : ____________
5. that cannot be forgotten : ____________

B. ***The word 'something' can be used as a Pronoun as well as an Adverb. Find out in the following sentences the part of speech of the word 'something'.***

1. Tony was something annoyed.
   (a) Adverb (b) Pronoun
2. The robber came out with something appearing sharp.
   (a) Adverb (b) Pronoun
3. She threw a wry glance at me, something between happiness and sadness.
   (a) Adverb (b) Pronoun
4. The boys were something frightened.
   (a) Adverb (b) Pronoun
5. I know something awful had happened to them.
   (a) Adverb (b) Pronoun
6. There were something like hundred girls in the garden.
   (a) Adverb (b) Pronoun

Unit 20

My Home and My Family

I PRE-READING EXERCISE

In the mighty march of civilization, man has moved from place to place in search of food and shelter which can secure him subsistence and security. So, man's home or living place or simply "place" is an important factor in human life.

There are many words showing "place". Match the columns 'A' and 'B' below.

Column A		Column B
1. hostel	(a)	home
2. creche	(b)	a place for soldiers
3. house	(c)	a place for hermits
4. shanty	(d)	a place for students
5. barracks	(e)	a crudely built living place
6. convent	(f)	a nursery for tiny tots
7. palace	(g)	a place for nuns
8. hermitage	(h)	a place for monks
9. monastery	(i)	a place for orphans
10. orphanage	(j)	a place for a royal family

II READING COMPREHENSION

Read the passage carefully.

It is a true saying

East or West,
Home is the best.

To me also, my home is the best place. Although I live in a small house situated on the outskirts of a city, yet I have so many advantages of it. The area around my house is a very clean one. You will not get a chance even once to point me out that you have to press your nose to avoid the foul smell while walking in the street in which my house is situated. Otherwise, in most of the areas of our country a person has not only to press his nose to avoid the foul smell but also close his eyes to avoid the frequent sights of heaps of garbage, step after step.

Just ask me the benefits of living in a good society around. When I come from my office in the evening, I find both of my sons playing in a park that is situated just in front of my house. When they see me, they run and say to me, "Good evening, papa". Can you imagine what I feel in those moments? I feel as if the two angels from the house of God had come down on the earth to love me forever. I find myself extremely happy. It is not just that they are very smart but the reality that thrills me is that they have learned while living in this locality the art of greeting their elders.

I still remember the situation only two years back when I lived in an unhealthy rural area. When I came back from my office in the evening, I found both of my sons playing marbles with the boys who started their every sentence with an abuse. Hence both of my sons also learned that art. The dust of the street covered their bodies like the snow on the mountains. It sometimes became difficult for me to recognize my own two sons.

But now I am happy because my wife has also learned the art of being a good housewife. When I enter the house, she takes my bag in her hand and puts it at the proper place. Then she gives me a glass of water and prepares a cup of tea for me.

She has dropped her old bad habit of searching my pockets for money and buying new sarees day after day. Now whenever I give her money to buy a saree or any cosmetics, she not only refuses to accept it but also tries to make me understand "Put by this money for these two angels".

Her soft voice allows me to keep my senses in order. Finally, I must admit I too have learned to be a good husband and a good father. I bring some beautiful toys and sweets and fruits for my children and sweet words and smiles for my wife as I return home from office.

However, I still often pity the rowdy people whom many abhor. I think, we can make them more civilized if we improve their surroundings and arrange good education, food and health measures and employment avenues for them.

Exercise 1

Understanding the passage

Put a tick mark (✓) against the true statement, and a cross mark (×) against the false statement.

1. The speaker does not like his own house. (   )

2. The speaker's house lies in the heart of a metropolis. ( )

3. The area around speaker's house is full of garbage and a foul smell often hovers over the locality. ( )

4. The speaker appears satisfied with the locality he is living in. ( )

5. When the speaker comes from his office in the evening, he finds both of his sons playing in the mud. ( )

6. When the sons of the speaker see their father in the evening, they wish him good evening. ( )

7. The speaker is thrilled because his sons have learned the art of greeting their elders. ( )

8. The speaker's wife has also become wiser now and she does not search her husband's pockets. ( )

9. The speaker's wife advises her husband to put by some money for their two sons. ( )

10. The speaker is not a good father because he brings no toys and fruits for his little ones. ( )

Exercise 2

Comprehension

A. ***Answer the following questions.***

1. What is the main advantage of living on the outskirts of a big city?

___

2. What are the advantages of living in a good society around?

3. Mostly how do the rural children behave with one another?

4. Often what kind of physical appearance do the rural children have?

5. What are the essential qualities of a good housewife in a lower middle class family?

6. How can rowdy people be made more civilized?

7. What changes have taken place in the behaviour of the members of speaker's family that have thrilled him?

B. ***Complete the following sentences.***

1. In a good society around, the children learn the art of

   ____ .

2. Where there are heaps of garbage, one has to cross the road by ________________________________ .

3. A married man feels happy if ____________________

   ____ .

4. In rural areas the children start their sentence with

   ____________________________ .

5. I bring some beautiful ________________________for my children__________________for my wife.

<u>Exercise 3</u>

Enrichment

Write down the textual words or phrases for the meanings given below.

1. outer area of a city : ____________________
2. benefits : ____________________
3. obnoxious : ____________________
4. call names : ____________________
5. lay by : ____________________
6. to identify : ____________________

Unit 21

Fashion and Simplicity

I PRE-READING EXERCISE

There are several words in the modern jargon which mean a place (often a fashionable one) for eating, meeting and purchase purpose. But almost always there is some difference in meaning. Please match the columns to distinguish between such different places.

1.	club	(a)	a sitting room in a private house
2.	cafeteria	(b)	an establishment providing accommodation and food for the travellers and tourists
3.	boutique	(c)	a small house
4.	parlour	(d)	the premises of an association dedicated to particular interest
5.	resort	(e)	a minor stopping-place
6.	hotel	(f)	a restaurant in which customers serve themselves from a counter and pay before eating
7.	halt	(g)	a night club
8.	cottage	(h)	a small restaurant selling light meals and drinks
9.	boite	(i)	a popular destination for holiday-makers
10.	cafe	(j)	a small shop selling fashionable clothes

II READING COMPREHENSION

Read the passage carefully.

In the modern society, we can see not only the youths but also the old ones practising fashions to attract the world. Fancy shows, beauty contests, etc. are being held in every corner of the world. Hence new and new fashions are being displayed throughout the world. There are so many fashion-designing institutes. It is the tailors' day.

People attend kitty parties, night clubs, etc. to expand their business connections and for that, they wear clothes of new styles or, we can say, they adopt new fashions that may or may not be of their own choice, but that are certainly expected to be appreciated by a large section of society. Hence even through fashions they are surrendering themselves to the materialistic world. Oh God! man has to play what sort of games to get a small room in the luxury compartment of the world!

On the other hand, a simple man who does not waste his time in getting ready for a kitty party or night club, or in other words, who does not surrender himself to materialism, remains bold and contented at every step of life. And here I would like to mention Mahatma Gandhi. He was a man with the simplest possible clothes but he had a courageous mind and had an invincible weapon of truth, candour, and non-violence. Most of the historical figures were the persons who believed in the principle of simplicity.

Simplicity is not just concerned with the outer personality of a person, but it is also related to one's simple and true ideas about certain aspects of life. A teacher can be said to be a totally simple one, when he or she not only wears simple clothes but also teaches his or her pupils the real meaning of life in a simple and precise manner.

Simplicity is also something concerned with a person's eating habits. A simple man takes simple but balanced diet. He never eats too much or, we can say, he does not believe in over-eating. Over-eating makes one fall a victim to many diseases. Besides, it may cause food shortage in a poor country like ours, all the vociferous glut notwithstanding.

A simple man believes in the principle of sacrifice and he remains ready for that in every walk of life. But what the modern man does, he does it for himself only. He takes rich diet and drinks excessively to remain a part of rich sections of society that can never like to be simple in any aspect of life.

It is a pity that nowadays it is a fashion to wear half or uglily clad in the name of fashion and to be boorish and churlish.

Exercise 1

Understanding the Passage

Put a tick mark (✓) against the true statement and a cross mark (×) against the false statement.

1. In the modern society, old people do not take any interest in fashions. ( )
2. Fancy shows, beauty contests, etc. are quite common things in the modern society. ( )
3. The modern time is the barber's day. ( )
4. People attend kitty parties, night clubs, etc. to show down their economic growth. ( )

5. Through fashions, we are surrendering ourselves to the materialistic world. ( )

6. A simple man remains bold and contented at every step. ( )

7. Mahatma Gandhi had a courageous mind and the invincible weapon of truth. ( )

8. A simple teacher wears simple clothes but he/she does not make the students aware of the real meaning of their life. ( )

9. A modern man believes in sacrifice. ( )

10. A modern man lives a happy and contented life.( )

Exercise 2

Comprehension

Answer the following questions.

1. Write down the life style of a modern man.

____

____

2. Wirte down the life style of a simple man.

____

____

3. Which life style would you prefer - the fashionable or the simple one and why?

____

____

4. Why do the rich people join the kitty parties, etc.?

___

___

5. How has the modern man surrendered himself to the materialistic world?

___

___

6. Explain how simplicity is the other name of patriotism. You may use your own imagination, if necessary.

___

___

___

7. What is, in author's opinion, the latest fashion these days?

___

___

B. ***Complete the following sentences.***

1. The modern man is displaying fashion because ______ ___ .

2. A simple man can be said to be a patriot because ______ ___ .

3. A simple man is always bold and contented because he remains laced with the weapons of ______

______________________________.

4. The rich section of the society can never be a simple one because ______________________________.
5. One can be a simple person by adopting ______________________________.

Exercise 3

Enrichment

Write down the textual words or phrases for the meanings given below.

1. present : ______________
2. make a prominent exhibition of (something) : ______________
3. too powerful to be defeated : ______________
4. candidness : ______________
5. scarcity : ______________

Unit 22

Leisure

I PRE-READING EXERCISE

There are different causes for different diseases. Some diseases are caused by bacteria. But there are many others which are caused by idleness or overwork, that is lack of leisure.

Please match the columns 'A' and 'B' below to give the exact meaning of each disease word.

	Column A		**Column B**
1.	alveolitis	(a)	loss of appetite
2.	amoebiasis	(b)	mental illness
3.	anorexia	(c)	infection with amoebas
4.	anosmia	(d)	loss of sleep
5.	insomnia	(e)	inflammation of the air sacs of the lungs
6.	anoxia	(f)	abnormally fast heart rate
7.	alopecia	(g)	loss of sense of smell
8.	bradycardia	(h)	loss of hair
9.	tachycardia	(i)	abnormally slow heart action
10.	neurosis	(j)	an absence of oxygen

II READING COMPREHENSION

Read the passage carefully.

The following two lines by Davies are known to every school child.

What is this life if full of care?
We have no time to stand and stare?

Man is practically a machine. Every machine needs rest for a while so as to do work for a long time in a precise way.

The whole day work makes a man tired and he feels a sort of boredom and wants to take a little leisure, so as to start again at his work with renewed energy.

The life of man has gone harder and more stressful in the modern age. It is found that the persons who do not take rest for the required period of time daily, fall victims to some serious diseases like high blood pressure, heart attack, nervous break down, etc.

In the modern times, men of upper classes have to do little physical work but they have to give more stress to their nerves to invent new ways to befool the people and to earn a lot of money.

The people working in factories, or doing any kind of physical work, need at least an hour's rest in the day to turn their minds towards something else which is quite different from the daily routine.

There are different ways of occupying one's leisure hours. One can adopt the method of collecting stamps, and coins. This kind of hobby provides the knowledge of different cultures of different countries. Hence through leisure one can enter a new world of knowledge.

Another method of spending one's leisure time usefully is gardening. This method develops new kind of emotions in the human mind. It also provides us some exercise. When we see the germination of seeds, the blooming of flowers and the attractive colours and softness of the newly born leaves, it generates in our heart a great love for nature. Thus, we learn to love nature and the whole plant kingdom as we love our little ones.

Another method of spending hours of leisure is to watch T.V. serials. It is a good method to get a great knowledge about the world around and for that we have 'the news' and general knowledge contests. We can see cricket matches, hockey matches, tennis matches and so. It all depends upon our tastes. We have different kinds of T.V. serials which give us slices of happiness and sorrow in their own styles. It is a popular and an easy method to utilize one's leisure usefully, as now, we have channels which provide us 24 hour service.

Exercise 1

Understanding the Passage

Put a tick mark (✓) against the true statement and a cross mark (×) against the false statement.

1. Man doesn't need any rest so as to do work for a long time in a precise way. (   )
2. Man doesn't need any leisure to regain energy. (   )
3. Rest for a required period of time daily is necessary to keep one's body fit. (   )
4. In the modern times, men of upper classes do more physical work than they do mental work. (   )

5. The labour classes working in factories, etc. do more hard physical work than the upper classes. ( )

6. By developing good hobbies like stamp collecting and coin collecting one can give rest to one's stressed nerves and limbs. ( )

7. Through gardening one can develop a number of emotions in one's heart. ( )

8. By watching T.V. serials, etc. one also feels happy and fresh. ( )

9. T.V. serials give us only slices of happiness. ( )

10. Even through leisure one can enter a new world of knowledge. ( )

Exercise 2

Comprehension

A. ***Answer the following questions.***

1. In what respect can man be compared to a machine?

____

____

2. Why is leisure necessary in the daily life of a person?

____

____

3. What kinds of diseases can excessively hard work and no rest cause to man?

____

____

4. Write down in three sentences some methods of spending leisure usefully. You may use your own imagination.

____

____

____

5. What is the main benefit of gardening? How does it generate love in our hearts?

____

____

6. What are the benefits of the T.V. to man?

____

____

B. ***Complete the following sentences.***

1. Men of upper classes give more stress to their nerves because ______________________________ .
2. A person doing hard physical work needs at least an hour's rest because ______________________ .
3. Gardening makes us learn to love nature when we see ______________________________________ .
4. On T.V. we can see ______________________________ .
5. The continuous work (without rest) makes a man _____ ______________________________________ .

Exercise 3

Enrichment

A. ***Write down the textual words or phrases for the meanings given below.***

1. free time for enjoyment : ____________________
2. ennui : ____________________
3. strain : ____________________
4. preys : ____________________
5. create or produce : ____________________

B. ***'Match the Columns' containing terms related to the flowers.***

1.	petals	(a)	having the stamens and other floral parts at the same level as the carpels
2.	corolla	(b)	having the stamens and other floral parts situated below the carpels
3.	stigma	(c)	the female part of a flower
4.	hypogynous	(d)	modified leaves of a flower which are usually coloured
5.	epigynous	(e)	the part of a pistal that receives the pollen during pollination
6.	perigynous	(f)	the petals of a flower whorl within the sepals
7.	gynandrous	(g)	having stamens and pistil united in onecolumn

Unit 23

J.L. Nehru

I PRE-READING EXERCISE

There are some people who are different from the common men in the sense that they cause or suffer violence or indulge in an unusual activity for their personal gain or for their country. Please match the columns to convey the correct meaning.

1.	soldier	(a)	a person who is killed because of his religious or other belief
2.	martyr	(b)	a person who collects secret information and conveys it to someone
3.	freedom-fighter	(c)	a soldier specially trained for carrying out raids
4.	pirate	(d)	a person who takes part in breaking into a house with an idea of stealing something
5.	robber	(e)	a person who commits robbery
6.	thief	(f)	a person who robs ships at the sea
7.	spy	(g)	a person who serves in an army
8.	commando	(h)	a person who takes part in a struggle (often violent) to achieve a political goal
9.	burglar	(i)	a person who steal things

II READING COMPREHENSION

Read the passage carefully.

India is a land of saints and leaders. J.L. Nehru was one of the most brilliant leaders of our country. He was the first Prime Minister of India.

He was born on 14th November, 1889. He was born with a silver spoon in his mouth. The name of his father was Motilal Nehru who was a leading lawyer. Mr. J.L. Nehru was brought up like a prince and was sent to England for higher studies. He got his degree in Law from England and returned to India as a Barrister.

J.L. Nehru was a peace-loving person who was very much impressed by the ideas of Mahatma Gandhi. So, he became a soldier in the freedom struggle. He adopted Gandhiji's way of peace and stubborn passive resistance against the British Government. He spent the prime of his life in jails. Mahatma Gandhi was also impressed by Nehru's way of working.

When India became independent, he was elected the Prime Minister of the country. Being a peace-loving person, he believed in honesty and had a great faith in the principles of Mahatma Gandhi. But he found the world different when China attacked India suddenly in September, 1962.

He was a great lover of children. They called him "Chacha Nehru". His birthday is still celebrated as "Children's Day".

The most important work that was done by him was the installation of heavy industry in India. He was determined that India should produce everything of need within the walls of the country. He wanted to make India a rich as well as self-dependent country.

He shaped the Indian history. Besides being a leader, he was a great writer and a great describer of history. He wrote down the 'Quit India Resolution' and was the author of the book 'Letters to a Daughter". He also wrote some other famous books like 'The Discovery of India', 'The Glimpses of World History', 'An Autobiography', etc. His keen interest in industrialization brought fruit for India when some steel plants were established successfully in India with the foreign help. He started the five-year plans. These five-year plans were a new kind of fight against poverty, hunger, disease, unemployment, etc. through which India was passing.

He proved that the help of the poor is the real worship of God. He worked for his countrymen tirelessly and he tried to establish peace in India and abroad.

He died on May 27, 1964. His name will remain shining like a star in the galaxy of great men in Indian History.

Exercise 1

Understanding the passage

Put a tick mark (✓) against a true statement and a cross mark (×) against a false statement.

1. Mr. J.L. Nehru was the first Prime Minister of India. ( )
2. Mr. J.L. Nehru was born on 16th November, 1889. ( )
3. Mr. J.L. Nehru was brought up like a common child. ( )
4. Mr. J.L. Nehru was a war-loving person. ( )

5. He adopted Gandhiji's way of peace and stubborn passive resistance against the British Government. (   )
6. China attacked India suddenly in September, 1962. (   )
7. Mr. J.L. Nehru was an eminent poet. (   )
8. Mr. J.L. Nehru was keen to see Indian industry at its acme. (   )
9. He started the five-year plans which were, indeed, a new kind of fight against poverty, hunger, unemployment, etc. (   )
10. Mr. J.L. Nehru wrote the famous books, 'The Discovery of India', 'The Glimpses of World History', 'An Autobiography', etc. (   )

<u>Exercise 2</u>

Comprehension

A. ***Answer the following questions.***

1. In what way was J.L. Nehru impressed by Mahatma Gandhi?

____

____

2. Why did the children call J.L. Nehru "Chacha Nehru"?

____

____

3. What did J.L. Nehru do for India?

____

____

4. Why did J.L. Nehru go to England and what was his achievement there?

____

____

5. Name some of the books which J.L. Nehru wrote.

____________________ ____________________

____________________ ____________________

6. What was Nehru's actual mission in starting the five year plans?

____

____

B. ***Complete the following sentences.***

1. J.L. Nehru was sent to England where he got __________

   ____ .

2. J.L. Nehru was greatly impressed by the ideas of Mahatma Gandhi. So, he ________________________

   ____ .

3. His main aim was to install ____________________ .

4. He wanted to make India a rich as well as ____________

   ____ .

5. He tried to establish __________________________

   ____ .

Exercise 3

Enrichment

A. ***Write down the textual words or phrases for the meanings given below.***

1. to be born in a rich family : ____________
2. inactive : ____________
3. obstinate : ____________
4. that which does not depend upon others : ____________
5. without taking rest : ____________

B. ***There are some people who are different from the common men. It is because of some peculiar inherent, inborn or acquired qualities, good or bad, in them***

Match the Columns to convey the correct meaning.

1.	leader	(a)	a woman seeking the right to vote through organized protest
2.	saint	(b)	a person living in solitude as a religious disciple
3.	suffragette	(c)	the person who leads a group
4.	usherette	(d)	a person who is regarded as being in heaven after death
5.	hermit	(e)	the head of an abbey of monks
6.	abbot	(f)	a woman who shows people to their seats in a theatre

Unit 24

Indo-Pak Relations

1 PRE-READING EXERCISE

Today, while considering a country's progress or her relations with other countries, it is not only her ability to fight a war which matters, but also her economic condition and the scientific advancement which she has made are regarded as significant. So, here are words concerned with different brands of science. Please match the Columns.

1. technology	(a)	the scientific study of animals
2. tribology	(b)	the scientific study of plants
3. zoology	(c)	the study of friction
4. demonology	(d)	the scientific study of animals
5. pharmacology	(e)	the scientific study of measurement
6. metrology	(f)	the application of scientific knowledge for practical purpose
7. dendrology	(g)	the branch of science concerned with the process and phenomena of atmosphere
8. meteorology	(h)	the branch of medicine which concernes with the action of drugs

II READING COMPREHENSION

Read the passage carefully.

The coming of Mr. Atal Behari Vajpayee as the new Prime Minister of India made Indians feel stronger. It was because of the new Prime Minister's avowed belief in strengthening India in the field of space technology and nuclearisation.

But like other Prime Ministers of India, he also fell in a state of dilemma whether India should start war with Pakistan or not, to stem Pakistan's evil machinations. Mr. Atal Behari Vajpayee having earlier showed great amount of faith in Pakistan felt at last compelled to say, "Pakistan has betrayed us and has attacked us in the garb of friendship. It has annexed Indian territory by violating the Line of Control". This is what he said while addressing local people and jawans soon after his arrival from Srinagar after the start of the Kargil Conflict.

Inspite of Vajpayee's best efforts like continuing the train 'Samjhauta Express' from Attari Border to Pakistan and starting of bus service from Delhi to Lahore, to develop friendly relations between the people of two nations, Pakistan could not be coaxed to friendly ways.

Pakistan continued sending mercenaries in the Indian territory. But for that India has gave her a befitting reply in Kargil. In this regard, when the then Pakistan's Foreign Minister Mr. Sartaj Aziz came to India, he was told clearly that if India had declared that it would not like to start the war first or it would not like to use the nuclear weapons first, it did not mean that it would allow Pakistan to use her nuclear weapons first. India has also declared not to use nuclear weapons against a non-nuclear country.

In his speeches, Mr. Atal Behari Vajpayee said, "Our land

has been captured by Pakistan. Continuous shelling has made thousands homeless. We will give a befitting reply". He also made it clear to the world the sort of game Pakistan was playing. Pakistan was trying to make the dispute of Jammu and Kashmir a religious issue, and in this regard he said, "we have more Muslims in India. In our country, all religions get equal opportunity but this is not the case in Pakistan".

Mr. Atal Behari Vajpayee told Mr. Sartaj Aziz, "We want peace but if war is imposed on us, the whole country is ready to face any situation".

So, it can be said here that India wants peace because war can lead to great destruction on both sides. It must be remembered: If peace is heaven, war is hell. War must be avoided as far as and as long as possible.

Exercise 1

Understanding the Passage

Put a tick mark (✓) against the true statement and a cross mark (×) against the false one.

1. Mr. Atal Behari Vajpayee took important steps in the fields of space technology and nuclearisation to make India a great power. ( )
2. Mr. Atal Behari Vajpayee showed a great faith in Pakistan. ( )
3. Pakistan is also willing to have friendship with India. ( )
4. The train 'Samjhauta Express' was started by the Pakistan government. ( )

5. Mercenaries in the Indian territory were not sent by Pakistan. ( )
6. More Muslims live in Pakistan than in India. ( )
7. India wants her occupied territory back from Pakistan in a peaceful manner which is quite possible. ( )
8. Mr. Vajpayee told Mr. Sartaj Aziz that India did not want war but if war was imposed on her, the whole country was ready to face any situation. ( )
9. India wants peace because war can lead to great destruction. ( )
10. War must be avoided as long as possible. ( )

Exercise 2

Comprehension

A. ***Answer the following questions.***

1. What was Mr. Vajpayee's dilemma?

____

____

2. What is India's policy in regard to use of nuclear weapons?

____

____

3. Why should India avoid war as far as possible?

____

____

4. What is the Line of Control (LoC) as far as Indo-Pak relations are concerned?

____

____

5. What efforts have been made by Mr. Atal Behari Vajpayee to develop friendly relations with Pakistan?

____

____

6. What did India make clear to the then Pakistan Foreign Minister in connection with the nuclear weapons?

____

____

7. If peace, what is war and why?

____

____

B. ***Complete the following sentences.***

1. Mr. Atal Behari Vajpayee made great efforts to develop friendly relations between two nations by _______________ .

2. Pakistan was trying to make _______________ .

3. The mercenaries sent to the Indian territory were given

____

4. Atal Behari Vajpayee said that we would not rest till the occupied territories ______________________.

5. We want peace but if war is imposed on us, ________ ____.

Exercise 3

Enrichment

A. ***Write down the textual words or phrases for the meanings given below.***

1. state of confusion : ______________
2. cheated : ______________
3. cajoled : ______________
4. taken illegaly : ______________
5. catastrophe : ______________

B. ***Give Antonyms of the following.***

1. progress : ______________
2. destruction : ______________
3. war : ______________
4. belief : ______________
5. dispute : ______________

Unit 25

Security in Villages

I PRE-READING EXERCISE

Throughout the history of mankind, man has shifted from place to place, mainly in search of security. Only in the modern times, the common man has got some security, so to speak. But unfortunately, still some time, this feeling of security is erased from the common man's mind by some forces. In certain rural areas, in particular, this feeling of security is still not quite strong. Although the people too have some responsibilities, yet the first duty of any government is to provide security to all the people. Now match the columns.

1.	massacre	(a)	the act of murdering an important person for political or religious reason
2.	catastrophe	(b)	slaughter on a mass scale by fire or nuclear weapons
3.	holocaust	(c)	an event of killing someone
4.	mishap	(d)	indiscriminate and brutal slaughter of people
5.	murder	(e)	an unlucky accident
6.	assassination	(f)	obeying the sentence of death on a condemned person
7.	stab	(g)	an event causing great destruction
8.	execution	(h)	a thrust with an edged weapon

II READING COMPREHENSION

Read the passage carefully.

India is a big country. Most of its population still lives in villages. Due to the slow industrial growth India still depends upon agriculture. The government often says that it would like to give more facilities to the villagers. But in the real sense, it is seen that the government is not very keen to protect the people living in the less crowded villages and no reforms have been done so far, at least not in all parts of the country.

Here is an example of a large massacre in the Kashmir Valley where a few foreign based terrorists gunned down 35 persons in the village Chatti Singhpora (Anantnag) on the evening of March 20, 2000. The date became important because the then US President Bill Clinton had only a day earlier (on 19th March) reached India on a state visit.

After this horrible incident a large number of leaders and bureaucrats rushed to the village. The villagers looked confused and perplexed. When they were asked about their future plan. They said, "we do not know what to do next. Some of the Central leaders have been here to console us and share our grief--"

For how long will these leaders and bureaucrats like to attend such funeral ceremonies instead of providing fool-proof security to the poor unprotected people in our country? Security should be beefed up in the villages, particularly in those which lie near the border areas.

As per press reports when the concerned authorities were asked about other problems regarding the reforms in the village, they said, "it is almost after 15 to 20 years that the village is getting so much attention from various government agencies. The water pipes are being laid after 15 years. The road, too, has been repaired, as some more VIPs are expected tomorrow"

Now our bureaucrats were watching face of one another and were feeling why they had been put such a difficult question.

The villagers further told that the terrorists were dressed in army uniforms and were carrying bottles of rum and were making a show of great mercy towards the villagers. The power supply was disconnected just 10 minutes before the catastrophe.

Can we imagine what freedom means to those who do not feel secure even more than five decades after independence?

This feeling of lack of individual security may be more pronounced in certain areas like Kashmir and Eastern states, but it is, more or less, very much there in most parts of our country. It is a matter which should make us sit up and compel us to ponder over it.

Exercise 1

Understanding the Passage

Put a tick mark (✓) against a true statement and a cross mark (×) against a false statement.

1. Most of the population of India lives in urban areas. (   )
2. In fact, the steps taken by our government for the progress of the ruralareas, are not sufficient. (   )
3. In the Kashmir Valley 35 persons were gunned down by the foreign based terrorists. (   )

4. The former U S President Mr. Bill Clinton arrived in India on 19th March, 2000. ( )
5. The villagers of Chatti Singhpora appeared confused and frightened. ( )
6. A battalion of bureaucrats rushed to the village. ( )
7. Security should not be beefed up in the villages, particularly in those which lie near the border areas. ( )
8. Our leaders and bureaucrats have a great experience of attending funeral ceremonies. ( )
9. The construction work was started in the village only when the arrivalof VIPs was expected in the near future. ( )
10. The terrorists were dressed in police uniform. ( )

Exercise 2

Comprehension

A. ***Answer the following questions.***

1. Why does India still depend upon agriculture?

____

2. Have reforms been done in the villages with full honesty?

____

____

3. What happened in the village Chatti Singhpora (Anantnag) in Kashmir?

____

4. How did a large number of leaders and bureaucrats behave after the mishap?

5. Why could the villagers of Chatti Singhpora not recognize the terrorists before the catastrophe?

6. Using your own ideas, write three sentences how security can be beefed up in villages near the border areas?

B. ***Complete the following sentences.***

1. ________________________ is a proof of lapse in security in the rural areas near the border.
2. The catastrophe of Chatti Singhpora had hammered the consciousness of villages and they were not ________________________.
3. The people of Chatti Singhpora looked ________________________.

4. A group of terrorists came ______________________________

____.

5. Slower industrial growth has forced India still to depend

____.

Exercise 3

Enrichment

A. ***Write down the textual words or Phrases for the meanings given below.***

1. slaughter : ______________
2. embarrassed : ______________
3. a great destruction : ______________
4. terrible : ______________
5. to tighten the security : ______________

B. ***'Un' and 'dis-' are prefixes.***

Now write down 'un-' or 'dis-' with the following words to convey the correct meaning. The first one has been done for you.

1. Not embarrassed un abashed
2. take a weapon away from ______arm
3. having no emphasis ______accented
4. fail to fulfil hopes ______appoint
5. refuse to show belief in something ______belief
6. fully in agreement ______animous

Unit 26

How I Celebrated My Last Birthday

I PRE-READING EXERCISE

Every child loves to celebrate his birthday as it probably seems to him the most important day of his life. In history certain years have great importance for different reasons. Match the columns 'A' and 'B' given below.

	Column A		Column B
1.	Third Battle of Panipat	(a)	1947
2.	The Battle of Buxar	(b)	1948
3.	Indian Independence Day	(c)	1761
4.	Gandhi-Irwin Pact	(d)	1994
5.	'Quit India' Movement	(e)	1999
6.	Assassination of Gandhiji	(f)	1764
7.	First General Election in India	(g)	1942
8.	GATT signed by India	(h)	1952
9.	PM's Bus Journey to Lahore	(i)	1931
10.	Mahatma Gandhi's Birth	(j)	1869

II READING COMPREHENSION

Read the passage carefully.

My birthday falls on the day when India got freedom, that is, 15th of August. I have always celebrated my birthday with my friends and with the members of my family. All of us sit together in the big hall of my house and then in the evening a cake is cut and everybody dances to the tunes of a light music.

The last year I turned twenty-one. As per previous practice, the big hall of my house was decorated with balloons and bunting. A big table was kept in the middle of the hall. Chairs were arranged in a large semi-circle. There was not much gathering in the hall.

In the evening I cut the cake. Everybody danced with the lilting music. It was night now. Everybody wanted to go back home. But all of a sudden my uncle who had been absent from the family for a long time entered the house. He showered great blessings on me and joined us in the celebration of my birthday.

To our surprise, he suddenly stopped the music and stood in the middle of the hall. Then he made an impassioned speech that I would never forget till my last breath. He said, "My dear little ones, as we know, Rohit is now twenty-one. This in a lay-man's language means that he is now an adult. Some may assign different ages to adulthood, but nobody can deny adulthood to a person who is twenty-one. That is why I say, Rohit is now undoubtedly an adult. Can any one among you tell me the real meaning of being an adult?"

There was a pindrop silence in the hall. "Let me tell you the responsibilities of an adult. At first a young boy tries to understand the problems of his own house. He looks with extra care whether the members of his family are fit as a fiddle. If he feels that any member of his family is suffering from some problem, then it is his first duty to solve his or her problem. Thus he gives support to his family. Now Rohit has arrived a stage from where if he opens his eyes properly, he will see so many domestic problems which he has to tackle with. It can be a turning point in his life if he learns the real art of living and that is to make sacrifices for others. He is now in the prime of his life. After solving the problems of his own house, he should try to solve the problems of his town, then of his country and his ultimate target should be the progress and well-being of the whole of mankind. For that he should be ready to make any sort of sacrifice. Don't mind me saying that this celebration of his birthday would be the last one. Now he should like to celebrate his birthday only on the day when he feels that there is not a single poor or miserable person in the world. Let nobody die of hunger, disease or want or neglect".

After saying this and other such platitudes, my uncle became silent. I felt upset at his remarks. I thought it was easy to say something big about the social reforms but it was a difficult task to give them a concrete shape.

I was keen to ask my uncle about his contribution to the reformation of society in his life. But my father who was also there told me that my uncle, that old fellow, had come to the town to donate his own house for the orphans to live in. I was told that he had already donated all his other possessions to the nation and had also signed a paper with the government that he would like to donate his eyes, kidneys, etc. after his death.

After staying for a short space of time, my uncle went out of the house even without taking a glass of water and vanished in darkness. I wonder if he will ever return! My heart has still not ceased praising him. I wonder if it was the celebration of my birthday in the real sense!

Exercise 1

Understanding the Passage

Put a tick mark (✓) against a true statement and a cross mark (×) against a false statement.

1. The speaker's birthday falls in the month of July. ( )
2. The speaker has always celebrated his birthday with his teachers. ( )
3. The big hall was decorated with balloons and bunting. ( )
4. A squarish table was kept in one corner of the hall. ( )
5. It is one of the important duties of an adult to serve his country. ( )
6. The speaker thought that it was easy to bring reforms in society. ( )
7. The speaker's father told him that his uncle had not yet decided to donate all his possessions to the nation. ( )
8. After some time, speaker's uncle wolfed down a box of pastries. ( )

9. The speaker was deeply impressed by his uncle. ( )

10. An adult is expected to shoulder a number of responsibilities of his family. ( )

Exercise 2

Comprehension

A. ***Answer the following questions.***

1. How did the speaker celebrate his brithday every year?

____

____

2. What kind of changes did the old man bring about in the birthday party?

____

____

3. Write down the main responsibilities of an adult, according to the old man.

____

____

4. Write down the sacrifices which the old man made for the welfare of society.

____

____

5. Which two impressions did the speaker form about his uncle?

(a) Earlier impression ______________________________

(b) Later impression ________________________________

6. When, according to the uncle, an adult should celebrate his birthday?

____

____

B. ***Complete the following sentences.***

1. The big hall of my house was ______________________

____.

2. The old man showered great blessings on me and ______

____.

3. The old man advised ___________________________

____.

4. It is an adult's major responsibility to _______________

____.

5. The main contribution of that old man to society was

____.

<u>**Exercise 3**</u>

Enrichment

A. ***Write down the textual words or phrases for the meanings given below.***

1. adorned : ____________________

2. graveyard silence : ______________

3. eager : ______________

4. quite fit : ______________

5. common sayings : ______________

B. ***Match the Columns below containing phrases and their meanings related to time.***

1.	ahead of time	(a)	do some job without wasting a moment
2.	behind time	(b)	out of date
3.	behind the times	(c)	at all times
4.	lose no time	(d)	earlier than expected
5.	time after time	(e)	with utmost speed, so as to finish before a specified time
6.	keep time	(f)	repeatedly
7.	against time	(g)	late
8.	all the time	(h)	rhythmically accompany

Unit 27

Travelling

I PRE-READING EXERCISE

There are several shades of people who leave their native place for a short period or for good. The aims of these people are different and so their periods of stay at the desired places are also different. Match the columns by drawing lines.

1.	pilgrim	(a)	a person who is travelling or visiting a place for pleasure
2.	tourist	(b)	a member of travelling people in the Indian subcontinent
3.	traveller	(c)	a person who often travels
4.	immigrant	(d)	a person who journeys to a holy place for religious reason
5.	emigrant	(e)	a person who wanders from place to place without a home or job
6.	gypsy	(f)	a member of people travelling from place to place on carts and having no permanent home
7.	vagabond	(g)	a person who comes to live permanently in a foreign country
8.	nomad	(h)	a person who leaves his own country to live permanently in another

II READING COMPREHENSION

Read the passage carefully.

Since ancient times, man has been travelling from place to place. We have had some well-known travellers like Fa-hian, T-Hieunsang, Ibn Batuta, Marco Polo and others. Their accounts tell us about many new things and places they visited. The adventures of Sinbad are also well-known. In literary books, we have several travellers who may just be only mythical characters.

Our ancestors started the system of pilgrimages. That was just a way of encouraging travelling. The purpose was not only religious but also recreational and even nationally cohesive. Then there were customs of visiting religious places on particular days or occasions or in the shape of fairs or melas. Some of them are still continuing, as for instance, the Kumbh Mela which is held every twelve years at Hardwar, Allahabad (Prayag) or some other place of religious importance. Bal Ganga Dhar Tilak started Ganesh Utsav to promote national integration. We have places of pilgrimage in all corners of our country like Dwarka in the west, Triputi in the south, Puri in the east and Amar Nath in the north.

Many people travel for sight-seeing. They love to see the beauties of nature. Many go to Kashmir for its beauty. People visit Shimla in winter to see the snowfall.

Some people visit certain places for adventure games. Others go just for business or trade. Indian coins have been found in South Asian countries, in western Asia and even in Italy and other European countries. It means India had trade relations with these countries in the past. Now in the modern times, when means of travel have greatly developed, many people visit several countries for trade purposes.

Travelling is a good means of increasing one's knowledge. Through the books, we can only imagine things, places and peoples. But when we actually visit particular places, we see things with our own eyes and meet different types of people and have face to face talk with them. Then we come to know the reality better which we cannot know even on the internet, as that is to a great extent formal and superficial.

Through means of travel, we can express our view-point to others in person and we can also know about others' view-point. We can know about different customs, languages, dresses, food-habits, and ways of living. In olden times, religions such as Christianity and Buddhism were spread by missionaries and preachers.

Now, students' tours go to different places to become bold, resourceful and more knowledgeable. Travelling at strange places brings in a person the spirit of adaptation, accommodation and toleration.

<u>**Exercise 1**</u>

Understanding the passage

Put a tick mark (✓) against the true statement and a cross mark (×) against the false statement.

1. Travelling was a part of the life with the ancient people and it still has an important role in the modern life. ( )
2. Our ancestors started the system of pilgrimages. ( )
3. The purpose behind the encouraging of travelling was not only religious but also

recreational and even nationally cohesive. ( )

4. Many of the fairs, etc. being held today, are directly related to the customs started by our ancestors. ( )
5. Mr. Subhash Chander Bose started Ganesh Utsav to promote national integration. ( )
6. We have different places where pilgrims from all corners of India come and meet one another. ( )
7. Indian coins have been found only in Italy. ( )
8. Through means of travel one can share one's ideas with different kindsof people coming from different states. ( )
9. In the modern times, the means of travel have shown a tremendous growth. ( )
10. The custom of travelling has lost its value because it is an expensive activity. ( )

Exercise 2

Comprehension

A. ***Answer the following questions.***

1. How does travelling improve our knowledge?

____

____

2. Why do people travel from one country to another?

____

____

3. What is the national importance of the Ganesh Utsav?

____

____

4. Why was the system of pilgrimages started?

____

____

5. How does travelling to a particular place differ from mere reading about it in a book?

____

____

6. How is travelling useful to students?

____

____

B. ***Complete the following sentences.***

1. Travelling offers an opportunity for exchanging _____ ____ .
2. Travelling makes a man courageous and __________ .
3. Travelling is an easy method to develop __________ ____ .
4. We have places of pilgrimage in all corners of our country like ______________________________ .
5. Through travelling we can know about different customs ____ .

Exercise 3

Enrichment

A. ***Write down the textual words or phrases for the meanings given below.***

1. very old : ____________
2. those who preach : ____________
3. facile : ____________
4. united : ____________

B. ***Certain words end in '-able' e.g. knowledgeable i.e. knowledge + able. Now add '-able' to the following words and also make other changes, where necessary, to get the correct word.***

1. use + able : ____________
2. hire + able : ____________
3. sale + able : ____________
4. duty + able : ____________
5. change + able : ____________
6. fly + able : ____________
7. forget + able : ____________
8. refer + able : ____________

C. ***Give Antonyms of the following.***

1. modern times : ____________
2. integration : ____________
3. beauty : ____________
4. encouraging : ____________

Unit 28

The Value of Friendship

I PRE-READING EXERCISE

There are among human beings true friends who have genuine affinity for each other or have identical views. But there may also be false friends who don't have this faculty in them. Similarly, certain words are identical in meaning while others are not. Please circle the word, which is different from the others in meaning in each set.

1. generous	:	magnanimous	:	lazy
2. transparent	:	translucent	:	opaque
3. tranquil	:	disturbed	:	calm
4. immortal	:	destructible	:	mortal
5. surprised	:	flabbergasted	:	happy
6. tiny	:	gigantic	:	titanic
7. comfort	:	anxiety	:	worry
8. gentle	:	intelligent	:	humble
9. opportunity	:	misfortune	:	adversity

II READING COMPREHENSION

Read the passage carefully.

"A friend in need is a friend, indeed", is an old saying. No doubt, "friend" is a sweet word. A friend may, sometimes be more valuable than a near relative. Whereas one's relatives often live at distant places, a friend may always be near at hand. So, in times of an emergency, whereas a relative may not be able to reach you to help you or take you out of the wood, a friend may do the job.

It is, indeed, deplorable that true friends are often not available these days. Most often we come across fair-weather friends who are not after you, but after your money, status, or position of which they take undue advantage. If you are by nature a gentle, generous, and accommodating one, it is a boon for them.

Where can now we find the example of a Krishna-Sudama friendship? As all of us have read and heard, Lord Krishna was a great king, besides being a prophet. Sudama was a poor Brahmin. Both studied together in their childhood. In later life, they parted their ways. But Krishna did not forget Sudama. He did not consider him an inferior being in spite of his glaring penury and he came to his help and rescue when all other doors had been closed on the poor Sudama.

The situation now is different. If you have money, you can have a swarm of well-wishers, friends, and parasites around you. As Davies tells in one of his poems entitled "Money", when he had money with him, his friends thronged him everywhere and all the time. Now when he has lost all his money, everybody has rejected and deserted him.

Is it necessary for man to have only a human being as his

friend? Some of the animals are better friends than men. Such are horses and dogs. It is proverbial about dog that he does not leave his master even if sure death stares him in the face.

Man can have books also as his true friends. Books are written by greatly learned people who have had great experience of life. They have embedded their gemmy ideas in their immortal works. Books give us ideas, views, and advice. They provide us guidance for success in life and tranquil, peaceful existence. They guide us on true path of life. They stand by us through thick and thin and never desert us in moments of adversity.

In spite of all this, nothing can be a substitute for a true and good human friend. A human being has emotions and feelings. He is not a dead matter. He can easily realize your worries and problems. He can appreciate your efforts and virtues. So, there is nothing in life like a true friend who always stands by you to advise you, encourage you, entertain you, help you and dissuade you, from going on a wrong path.

<u>**Exercise 1**</u>

Understanding the passage

Put a tick mark (✓) against the true statement and a cross mark (×) against the false statement.

1. A friend can never be as valuable as one's relatives can be. ( )
2. In the modern times, most of our friends are fair-weather friends. ( )
3. The modern friends take much advantage of

one's generosity and humble nature. ( )

4. Money is a magnet for the false well-wishers and fair-weather friends. ( )
5. Sometimes, dogs and horses prove better friends than human beings. ( )
6. Books cannot be our friends. ( )
7. Books provide us guidance for success in life and tranquil, peaceful existence. ( )
8. Blessed is the man who has some true and honest friends in the shape of human beings. ( )
9. Only a human being can understand you, for he has emotions and ideas within him. ( )
10. A good and sincere friend will not ever dissuade you from doing anything wrong. ( )

Exercise 2

Comprehension

A. ***Answer the following questions.***

1. Explain the point that sometimes friends are more valuable than a real relative.

____

____

2. Explain who is a fair-weather friend.

____

____

3. On what basis can one say that the friendship of Lord Krishna and Sudama was a real one?

____

____

4. What kinds of things can also be friends to a man?

____

____

5. What are the main qualities which should be there in a true friend?

____

____

6. What was Davies' experience with his friends?

____

____

B. ***Complete the following sentences.***

1. The books can be our true guides as they ____________
____ .

2. Nothing can be a substitute for a true friend because
____ .

3. A true friend appreciates your ____________________ .

4. A true friend dissuades you from __________________ .

5. The modern society is full of ____________________ .

Exercise 3

Enrichment

A. ***Write down the textual words or phrases for the meanings given below.***

1. truly : ____________
2. poverty : ____________
3. one who wishes well : ____________
4. precious : ____________
5. calamity : ____________

B. ***The compound word 'well-wisher' makes its plural by adding '-s' to its last element i.e. well-wisher (singular) — well-wishers (plural). But there are some words in case of which '-s' is added to the first element or to both the elements of the word. Now, convert the following singular nouns into plural nouns.***

Singular		Plural
1. Governor-General	:	____________
2. man-of-war	:	____________
3. passer-by	:	____________
4. sister-in-law	:	____________
5. looker-on	:	____________
6. woman-servant:	:	____________
7. Lord-justice	:	____________
8. story-teller	:	____________

Unit 29

Price Rise in India

I PRE-READING EXERCISE

Modern age is the age of Economics. We find words pertaining to this subject wherever we go. Some of the words are identical in meaning while others are different. Here are some simple words. Please circle the word which is different in meaning from the others, in each set.

1.	consumption	:	combustion	:	burning
2.	enforce	:	impose	:	allow
3.	dependable	:	trustworthy	:	dependent
4.	stable	:	firm	:	shaky
5.	wicked	:	atrocious	:	humble
6.	expenditure	:	expenses	:	accounts
7.	lavish	:	luxurious	:	odorous
8.	frequent	:	occasional	:	seldom
9.	burgeoning	:	flourishing	:	decreasing

II READING COMPREHENSION

Read the passage carefully.

India being an over-populated country, the consumption of everything here is on a large-scale. But, the government of this country remains highly under pressure because a large part of its funds goes in paying salaries and allowances to bureaucrats and legislators. So, the government imposes new taxes on the industrial goods and also gives the support prices to the crops produced by the farmers. All this causes a rise in the prices of articles.

Rise in prices of luxury goods does not concern the common man. But, the common man is passing through a rough weather as the prices of many consumer goods and necessaries like food, clothing, and things of every day use are also showing an upward trend.

The other main factor is the rise in the prices of petroleum roducts in the international market. As we know, India is mainly dependent on the Gulf countries for petroleum products. When there is a rise in the prices of petrol, diesel etc., the government has to increase the fares and freights of trains, buses, aeroplanes, ships, etc. but all the expenses in the long run are to be borne by the common man. The companies increase the prices of their products to equalize the taxes and increased fares and freights.

The prices of the crops are also not stable. It is because of the sharp rise in the prices of fertilizers, seeds, pesticides, and other agricultural inputs. This has affected the petty farmers. They can hardly get the reasonable return for their produce. Hence they every year cry hoarse to the government to increase the support prices of wheat, rice, sugarcane, etc. produced by them. To some extent, their demand is genuine.

Sometimes, the crafty businessmen take the bureaucrats in the net of their atrocious tactics and by storing several products of daily use, they create an artificial shortage. As the demand of a product increases or remains as it is in the market, its price increases. But on the other hand, even in times of shortage, one may get that very thing in the black-market.

During the days of elections different parties accept money from the businessmen and big business houses to meet their election expenses. Whichever party comes in power, allows the manufacturers to raise the prices of their products. Unfortunately, there is virtually no government control over prices and the common man with limited income, has to beat his breast day in and day out.

Another important factor for price rise is the lavish inflow of black money. The rich people have two kinds of income. One that they show in their accounts and the other that they do not show in their accounts and this latter type of income is known as black money. This also leads to increase in prices.

The policy of deficit financing by the government is also responsible for the rise in prices. Deficit financing leads to increase in circulation of money in the shape of currency notes. It means money is in excess but things are in shortage. This leads to rise in prices.

Some of the other factors that cause price rise are faulty taxation system, inflation, frequent increase in salaries and perks to employees, wastage, expenditure on luxuries, over-staffing in offices, etc. Prices can be kept under control if the government and people work with co-operation. Banks and some other government departments and PSU's have now started attractive Voluntary Retirement Scheme (VRS) and Gold Handshake to curtail the staff.

Droughts and floods also lead to fall in production. Strikes and lock-outs should also be avoided to increase production. Strict laws should be passed and implemented against hoarding, black-marketing, and tax evasion. Above all, effective steps should be taken to control the burgeoning population which has nullified all our progress.

Exercise 1

Understanding the passage

Put a tick mark (✓) against the true statement and cross mark (×) against the false statement.

1. Though India is a densely populated country yet the consumption of essential items is not much there. ( )
2. The Indian government always remains under pressure because a large part of its funds goes in paying salaries to the bureaucrats and legislators. ( )
3. When the prices of luxury goods increase, it is the common man who is badly hit. ( )
4. The rise in prices of essential goods is directly related to the prices of petroleum products. ( )
5. In India there is a great stability in the prices of agricultural products. ( )
6. Some businessmen take bureaucrats in their net and by hoarding products, they create a shortage of the goods in the market for a short time. ( )

7. Mostly the rich people have two kinds of income. ( )

8. India has to face droughts and floods in some of its regions almost every year. ( )

9. Prices of essential goods can be kept under control if the government and people work with co-operation. ( )

10. The burgeoning population has wiped away all our progress. ( )

<u>Exercise 2</u>

Comprehension

A. ***Answer the following questions.***

1. How does the burgeoning population of our country affect our economy?

____

____

2. What are the main causes of increase in prices of essential goods?

____

____

3. What are the factors responsible for the rise in the prices of crops?

____

____

4. What do you know about black money?

____

____

5. How can the prices of essential goods be stabilized in India?

____

____

6. Can you write a few words about the process of curtailing staff in offices, etc.?

____

____

B. ***Complete the following sentences.***

1. The rise in rates of fares and freights are indirectly paid by________________ through____________________.
2. Increase in support prices of the crops causes ________ ____.
3. Artificial shortage of essential goods is caused by ____.
4. The big business houses help the politicians during elections and they in turn help them by ___________ ____.
5. Banks and some government departments have now started ______________________________________.

Exercise 3

Enrichment

A. ***Write down the textual words or phrases for the meanings given below.***

1. expenditure : ________________
2. cunning : ________________
3. excessive or generous : ________________
4. causes : ________________
5. false : ________________

B. ***Give the Antonyms of the following.***

1. stable : ________________
2. increase : ________________
3. important : ________________
4. atrocious : ________________
5. reasonable : ________________

Unit 30

My Pet

I PRE-READING EXERCISE

Children's pets have certain characteristics which we realize but sometimes fail to observe. Match the Columns 'A' and 'B' to distinguish between different characteristics pertaining to pets.

Column A		Column B
1. cute	(a)	strong
2. exotic	(b)	substantial (money etc.)
3. robust	(c)	attractive in an attractive way
4. handsome	(d)	easy to mould or cut
5. soft	(e)	short and sturdy (person)
6. flexible	(f)	attractive for being colourful
7. cosy	(g)	rounded and plump
8. chunky	(h)	giving a feeling of comfort and warmth
9. chubby	(i)	easy to bend without breaking

II READING COMPREHENSION

Read the passage carefully.

I have a pet, named Jimmy. About a month back it was a lean and feeble creature. It walked with a limp. Sometimes it wiggled its left hind toe while walking. It remained unaware of its main responsibility and sneaked out of the main gate to play in the street.

But gradually, a sort of intelligence developed in it as it began to eat selective items. In a few days, it ballooned up. Now it does not go into the street to move about. It does not take part in rooting around for bones and scraps like stray dogs.

It is a cute dog, which seldom barks. It likes to live inside the house. It has learned the art of safeguarding its master's house against the burglars.

It enjoys itself sprightly as I give it its daily bath. Then I comb its hair. It sits on its bed, wagging its tail. Throughout the process, a wave of love seems to run through its eyes.

It daily goes out for an evening walk with me. On the way, it does not allow any other dog to boss it about. The stray dogs take to their heels when it wuffs.

It does not bite anybody but barks at (him) when it finds him doing something wrong. It has been inoculated against many fatal diseases.

It has become so wise that it does not uproot even the small plants and flowers in the lawn. It does no harm to vegetables in the kitchen garden. It observes the things happening around with great alertness. Sometimes, it barks at certain things. Perhaps it wants to express its own views. But it becomes quiet after a few moments realizing its language problem.

I love it very much. That is why it sleeps with me at night for sometime. Then it sneaks out of the door in the porch, and moves around to watch its master and his house. What an example of being true to one's salt!

Exercise 1

Understanding the passage

Put a tick mark (✓) against the true statement and a cross mark (×) against the false statement.

1. Jimmy wiggled its left hind toe while walking because it was a strong dog. ( )
2. In the beginning Jimmy was quite aware of its main responsibilities. ( )
3. Jimmy ballooned up when it started eating selective items. ( )
4. Now Jimmy does not take part in rooting around for bones and scraps like stray dogs. ( )
5. Jimmy barks day and night. ( )
6. Jimmy combs its hair itself. ( )
7. Jimmy has not been inoculated against many fatal diseases. ( )
8. Jimmy barks when it has to express itself. ( )
9. The whole night it sleeps with me. ( )
10. It is a sign of its being an intelligent creature as it does not uproot even small plants and flowers

in the lawn. ( )

Exercise 2

Comprehension

A. ***Answer the following questions.***

1. Describe Jimmy's condition a month back.

____

____

2. What bad habits has Jimmy left?

____

____

3. Write about Jimmy's good habits.

____

____

4. How do you know that Jimmy loves you very much?

____

____

5. What things prove that Jimmy is a responsible dog and is true to its master's salt?

____

____

6. Name any four animals and/or birds which you think are true to their salt.

1. ________________ 2. ________________

3. ________________ 4. ________________

B. ***Complete the following sentences.***

1. Being a lean and feeble creature Jimmy walked ________

   ____.
2. It does not take part in rooting ____________________

   ____.
3. After its bath, it sits on its bed and wags its tail when I

   ____.
4. It is true to its master's salt because ________________

   ____.
5. Sometimes, it barks at certain things ________________

   but ______________________________________.

Exercise 3

Enrichment

A. ***Write down the textual words or phrases for the meanings given below.***

1. weak : __________________
2. thin : __________________
3. unconscious : __________________
4. become fat, plump, or swollen : __________________
5. injected : __________________

B. ***Give Antonyms of the following words.***

1. lean : __________________
2. safeguard : __________________

Unit 31

Planets and Stars

I PRE-READING EXERCISE

Space research and technology have gained great prominence since the last quarter of the last century, as man is at present more inquisitive about the formation, shape and structure of the heavenly bodies than ever before.

The following are some words in column 'A' connected with space. Match the columns 'A' and 'B' to know the correct meaning of each word.

1.	planet	(a)	a person trained to travel or fly in space
2.	star	(b)	an artificial satellite used as a base for manned operations in space
3.	spacecraft	(c)	a ball of burning gases in the space
4.	space station	(d)	an artificial body put in orbit to move round the earth
5.	astronaut	(e)	a vehicle used for travelling in space
6.	rocket	(f)	heavenly body revolving round the sun, having no light of its own
7.	satellite	(g)	a cylindrical projectile which can be sent at a great height in space by the combustion of fuel

II READING COMPREHENSION

Read the passage carefully.

The main difference between a planet and a star is that a planet has a surface as our earth has but a star is a burning ball of gases like the sun. Let us consider what the moon is. The moon is a satellite which revolves round the earth. The human life is not possible on the moon. It is because it has a very low gravitational pull. So, the water and oxygen cannot stay on the surface of the moon.

There are nine planets in total that revolve round the sun. None of them has light of its own. The moon shines as she gives out the light borrowed from the sun. The Jupiter is the biggest among all these and the Pluto is the smallest one.

It has been found that the soil of the moon is of smoky colour. The chief content in it is the rocks. So, the soil of the moon is lacking in fertile contents. Hence the moon can be called barren land.

If we go still higher in the sky, we would be astonished to find the stars hundreds of times bigger than our sun.

Some stars have got extinguished with the passage of time but their light is still reaching the earth's surface because it travelled from them long long ago. We have invisible stars, which emit no light as they are made of certain kind of invisible mass.

We have black holes which look like a football in size and shape but may have a gravitational pull even greater than that of our earth. Hence they sometimes devour the little stars which enter their gravitational field.

If we look at the sky through a powerful telescope, out mind will boggle at the sight of squillions of tiny balls which shine constantly or give our light that flickers moment after moment.

If you have learned all this, take a fresh assignment to learn more. After learning that, take another assignment and so on, because knowledge has no limit like the sky. That is why sometimes we say about a thing which is infinite or limitless that "sky is the limit". So, we can call knowledge "the sky on the earth" and that can be the message from the sky, the planets, and the stars.

Exercise 1

Understanding the Passage

Put a tick mark (✓) against the true statement and a cross mark (×) against the false statement.

1. The main difference between a planet and a star is that a planet revolves round the sun while a star is a stationary object. ( )
2. The moon is a satellite. ( )
3. The moon has a great gravitational pull. ( )
4. There are eight planets in total that revolve round the sun. ( )
5. The Jupiter is the biggest planet. ( )
6. The sun is the biggest star in the universe. ( )
7. There cannot be an invisible star in the universe.( )
8. A black hole looks like a football in size and

shape but it may have a gravitational pull even greater than that of our earth. ( )

9. There are squillions of stars across the sky. ( )

10. All stars have similar shape and size. ( )

Exercise 2

Comprehension

A. ***Answer the following questions.***

1. What is a planet?

____

____

2. What is a star?

____

____

3. Why is the moon said to be 'barren land'?

____

____

4. Why is the light of some stars still reaching the earth's surface while they have got extinguished with the passage of time?

____

____

5. What is a black hole in the sky?

____

____

6. Using your imagination and on the basis of your reading of the passage, write three sentences on "Sky is the Limit".

____

____

B. ***Complete the following sentences.***

1. Our mind boggles at the sight of ________________

____.

2. The moon is a satellite which ________________

____.

3. The sun is a star because ________________

____.

4. We have stars even bigger ________________

____.

5. Human life is not possible on the moon because ______

____.

Exercise 3

Enrichment

A. ***Write down the textual words or phrases for the meanings given below.***

1. power of attraction of the earth : ________________

2. light not of one's own : ______________

3. surprised : ______________

4. not visible : ______________

5. swallow : ______________

B. ***Fill in the blanks with 'l' or 'll' to form a correct word. The first one has been done for you.***

1. a sharp rattling sound = bratt l e
2. to swing back and forth = osci – ate
3. to whip or flog = flage – ate
4. made of wool = woo – y
5. grasp tightly with one's hand = c – asp
6. a loud and confused noise = c – amour
7. flattened circle = e – ipse
8. of various kind = misce – aneous

C. ***Give Antonyms of the following words by adding prefixes 'de-' or 'mis-'.***

1. conduct : ______________
2. behave : ______________
3. manage : ______________
4. fuse : ______________

Unit 32

Western Culture and Life Style

I PRE-READING EXERCISE

Sometimes a word has different connotations in different contents. Take for example, the simple word "wing". In general, this word "wing" invokes in our mind the image of a bird. But we only rarely pause to ponder that the word is related to human life in more than one ways. Match the Columns given below.

1.	in the wings	(a)	in flight
2.	on the wing	(b)	a state of happiness
3.	on a wing and a prayer	(c)	fly away
4.	on wings	(d)	ready to do something
5.	spread one's wings	(e)	act without preparation
6.	take wing	(f)	with only the slightest chance of success
7.	wing it	(g)	left / right part of a building
8.	under one's wing	(h)	extend one's activities or business etc.
9.	take to the wings up	(i)	fly in the sky
10.	left/ right wing (of a building)	(j)	into one's protective care

II READING COMPREHENSION

Read the passage carefully.

It is a common belief that without money nothing is possible in the modern era. It is so because the MNCs (multinational companies) are spreading their wings in every field in India.

So, we have in our country all things from a pin to an aeroplane made by some foreign company. In the glitter of foreign life, which is based on the manipulation of money instead of real friendship or real love between human hearts, the Indians are also losing their cultural shape to some extent. This is bringing about a number of changes in our living styles.

In the name of globalisation we are being sold foreign branded sweetened water in the form of cold drinks, sweet things like biscuits made of wheat, tinned fruits, vegetables, pickles, jams, concentrated fruit juices, chocolates, etc. All these things are produced in India. For that, the foreign companies buy raw material at low rates in India, process it in India and then sell the manufactured products to the Indians at a very high price. Previously, the Britishers took the raw material from India, changed it into finished goods and sold it back to the Indians at exorbitant rates. Now, the foreigners need not take the raw material to their own countries when they can do the mischief on our own land and thus beat us in our own house.

Isn't it to say in a layman's language that our own shoes are beating our own heads?

To make themselves counted among those duped and desperate buyers of such things, many of our brothers have doubled their struggle and many others among us have adopted a motto to earn money by hook or by crook that is, by duping and cheating their own compatriots, just to fill the coffers of the foreigners. Hell to all honesty just for the palate and that at the cost of our poor nation! So, in the long run we are making our brothers corrupt and criminals forever. Because of these delicacies which are only for the rich, prices of the raw things like vegetables, fruits and milk sky-rocket in the market and the poor can buy neither the delicacies nor even the raw food items.

We are also being sold cars of different brands as well as other luxury items which are bringing frustration and poverty to our own people in several ways. To get such things a few of us are moving heaven and earth to corner money somehow. Thus even unwillingly we make ourselves slaves of these modern giants who have financial means to hold the neck of a poor nation like India.

On the other hand a few of our own companies like Wipro, Ranbaxy, Cipla, Infosys, Satyam Computer, Reliance Industries and Pantafour, etc. have now done quite well even abroad kudos to such Indian enterprises!

Thus we are selling new technology and medicines to save the so called precious lives of the foreigners but are buying sweet water and a few luxury items that would ruin us in the long run and would bring ultimately death to a great nation like India.

The western culture has entered every part of our life-style. Our food habits, dress, music, song, dance, behaviour in society, our treatment of our brothers, relations and friends have all got a sea-change. For instance, we have lost all regard for our elders and have no sympathy for our poor relations. Thus, virtually our materialistic malady or ecstasy has almost touched dizzy heights.

The best thing for us is to accept all that is good in the western culture without giving up the good things in our own culture instead of going the whole hog for the western culture. Even the Vedas say that we should accept good ideas from wherever they come:

Let noble thoughts come to me from every side.

Gandhiji said that we should keep the doors and windows of our house open so that fresh wind may enter from any side.

So, we should not reject western culture altogether but adopt its good points only which are in tune with the spirit of our own culture and society.

Exercise 1

Understanding the Passage

Put a tick mark (✓) against the true statement and a cross mark (×) against the false statement.

1. MNCs are facing a stiff competition in India. ( )
2. In India we have only the aircrafts which are the products of MNCs. ( )
3. In the glitter of foreign life, Indians too are losing their real shape and are adopting the foreign life style. ( )
4. In order to buy luxuries many Indians have geared up their struggle and many others have adopted a motto to earn money by hook or by crook. ( )
5. The lust for luxuries is making our society a peaceful and honest one. ( )

6. The MNCs get the required raw material from our own country at a cheaper price and sell it at high prices as finished goods. (   )
7. Some of our companies are selling new technology life saving drugs abroad. (   )
8. We should accept all kinds of products, that have been produced by the MNCs. (   )
9. Even the Vedas say that we should accept good ideas from wherever they come. (   )
10. So, we should reject western culture altogether. (   )

Exercise 2

Comprehension

A. ***Answer the following questions.***

1. According to the author what do the MNCs (Multinational Companies) do in India?

   ____

   ____

2. Write down the names of four Indian companies which have done well abroad?

   A. ____________________ B. ____________________

   C. ____________________ D. ____________________

3. In what respects has the western culture affected the Indian way of life?

   ____

   ____

4. What should be our real attitude to the western culture?

____

____

5. Don't you find a contradiction in the author's thinking when he praises the Indian companies going abroad but condemns the foreign companies operating in India? Give your own views with reasons.

____

____

____

____

6. Give two examples to illustrate that crass apathy has penetrated our souls. Restrict your answer to the lesson only.

____

____

B. ***Complete the following sentences.***

1. A great nation like India is dying because of the purchase of _______________________________.

2. We should not reject western culture altogether but adopt its _______________________________.

3. Thus we are selling new technology and medicines to save the so-called precious lives of the foreigners but are buying sweet water and a few luxury items that

would ____.

4. It is the belief of the common people that without money nothing is possible in the modern era. It is so because the MNCs are spreading ______________________________

____.

Exercise 3

Enrichment

Write down other words or phrases for those given below.

1. manipulation of money : ____________________
2. spreading their wings : ____________________
3. in the long run : ____________________
4. frustration : ____________________
5. in tune : ____________________
6. to move heaven and earth : ____________________
7. dizzy heights : ____________________

Unit 33

God Helps Those Who Help Themselves

I PRE-READING EXERCISE

We, as human beings, are a homogeneous and heterogeneous mixture of so many disparate elements, not only physically but also intellectually and spiritually. Often, divine, supernatural, religious, artistic and mythological words and terms get mixed up in our thinking, conversation and writings. Match the Columns given below.

1. God	(a)	an angel, associated with light
2. muse	(b)	a person living in solitude as a religious discipline
3. ghost	(c)	a person regarded as an inspired teacher or proclaimer of the will of God
4. seraph	(d)	a religious recluse
5. sage	(e)	ruler of the universe
6. hermit	(f)	a profoundly wise man
7. anchorite	(g)	any of the nine goddesses who encouraged and protected poetry, music, etc. (believed by the ancient Greeks)
8. prophet	(h)	an ordained minister of the catholic
9. priest	(i)	an apparition of a dead person which is believed to appear

II READING COMPREHENSION

Read the passage carefully.

It may seem a cliche or platitude to say but in practical life, it is still a true saying that God helps those who help themselves. One may be regular and punctual in worshipping God and may be going to a religious place regularly. But it is a fact that to earn one's bread and butter or to do one's other jobs related to one's business, it needs a self-attempt. Even Lord Krishna conveyed his message through the Gita, "One should continue doing one's duty but the fruit of one's struggle is in the hands of God." One can learn a good lesson from this message. It is that one should do hard work but not expect any fruit. Let the fruit, if any, come itself or by grace of God, so to say.

A student cannot hope to pass an examination without making a hard preparation for it. He may be a theist and good worshipper of God. Most religious preachers rightly say that God will not help that person who does not take interest in doing his own work and who tries to put all his responsibilities on the shoulders of God or his fellow-beings.

God likes only those who have true faith in the principle of doing their own work themselves. Hence they say that man should do his every small or big job with his own hands and mind instead of depending on others to do so for him.

As a by-product, it will also help in ending poverty and slavery or bonded labour to some extent. It is so because the poor sections will no longer think of working only as slaves and servants. They will instead pay attention to health, education and higher values of life. They will try to raise their standard of living. The rich will also learn to give up sloth.

The habit of self-help in different walks of life makes a man courageous and self-confident and also brings good wishes for him from a large number of people in society. The annals of History are filled with the glorious and courageous deeds of those people who adopted the principle of self-help.

It is also seen that a hard-working man has an immense sense of self-respect. Perhaps that is why even a handicapped person tries his best to earn his own bread and butter instead of depending on others.

Those who are still wandering in some other imaginary world and have not so far learned the art of doing their work with their own hands, should learn it from the little insects like ants and bees which always keep themselves busy.

Animals and birds also do their jobs with their own efforts. They never try to make others their slaves and they never depend on others for their food. It is because they instinctively believe in the principle of self service or self-help.

Exercise 1

Understanding the Passage

Put a tick mark (✓) against the true statement and a cross mark (×) against the false statement.

1. One who regularly and punctually worships God gets his every job done without doing any efforts. ( )
2. Lord Krishna conveyed his message through the Gita, "One should continue doing one's duty

but the fruit of one's struggle is in the hands of God" ( )

3. Most religious preachers condemn the theory that God helps those who help themselves. ( )
4. The spirit of self-service will help in ending poverty and slavery or bonded labour to some extent. ( )
5. The spirit of self-service will also make the rich give up sloth. ( )
6. A self-helper is not liked in any society. ( )
7. A self-helper cannot attain qualities like self-confidence and courage. ( )
8. It is a must for a self-respected person that he should have the quality of self-help. ( )
9. Animals and birds also do their jobs with their own efforts. ( )
10. A person who is not willing to obey the principle of self-help definitely needs some slaves to help him at every step of life. ( )

Exercise 2

Comprehension

A. ***Answer the following questions.***

1. What message did Lord Krishna convey to the world?

___

___

2. Whom does God love?

____

____

3. What sort of lesson can be learned from ants, birds, and animals?

____

____

4. How can one see the end of slavery across the world?

____

____

5. How can self-help help in ending poverty and slavery?

____

____

6. Write three sentences on "Religion and the Principle of Self-help".

____

____

____

B. ***Complete the following sentences.***

1. We can earn our bread and butter only if we are ______
________________________________.

2. Even a theist cannot pass the examination if ________
________________________________.

3. The habit of self-help makes a man ________________

____.

4. The quality of self-help ______________________

____.

5. Self-help is a method to end the institution of ________

____.

Exercise 3

Enrichment

A. ***Write down other words or phrases for those given below.***

1. one who believes in the existence of God : ________________
2. devotee : ________________
3. bold : ________________
4. at a particular time : ________________
5. without failure : ________________

B. ***Give Antonyms of the following.***

1. theist : ________________
2. cephalous : ________________
3. compose : ________________
4. moral : ________________
5. fuse : ________________
6. populate : ________________

Unit 34

Of Telecom and Stocks

I PRE-READING EXERCISE

It is rightly said that the Indian superiority in the field of Information Technology has emerged because of the underlying fact that Indian mind is specifically suited to the grasping of intricacies of mathematics – a subject which is stated to have originated in India. No doubt, counting is an important factor in all branches of modern knowledge. Match the Columns given below.

Column A		Column B
1. million	(a)	an indefinite large number
2. billion	(b)	large
3. trillion	(c)	10^9
4. squillion	(d)	10^6
5. giga	(e)	single
6. mega	(f)	10^{12}
7. micro	(g)	denoting a factor of 2^{30}
8. mono	(h)	partial
9. mero	(i)	small

II READING COMPREHENSION

Read the passage carefully.

Concerning the Indian economy the Prime Minister Atal Behari Vajpayee said to the Press on April 29, 2000, "We will pursue with policies which will enable us to realise our full potential. These include fiscal consolidation, reforms of banks and financial institutions, credible disinvestment programme and removal of infrastructure bottlenecks".

Thus Mr. Vajpayee gave stress on developing the infrastructure in India in a big way. Running on the same lines, Finance Minister, Mr. Yashwant Sinha, also explained to the Press in Asian Development Bank's high level round-table meeting, "It is estimated that 75 million telephone connections would be required by 2005 and 175 millions by 2010. At current prices, this translates into an additional investment of nearly $ 37 billions by 2005 and $ 70 billions by 2010." Needless to say that the commonest must also have telephone connection to ensure real growth. Even the American President, Bill Clinton, who visited India in March 2000, declared that Information Technology and Telecommunication were the key to the removal of poverty in India.

So much for the Telecom industry, though much more can be said. But another point here is that of the stock market. The stock market is often said to be the index of a country's economy. But, unfortunately, this does not happen in India. It is because high level corruption prevails in our country of which the stock market is the living example. The Mumbai Stock Exchange crashed precariously in the wake of the Budget proposals for 2001 and the Kolkata Stock Exchange even presented the payment problem.

Most of the black money is invested in the stock market . Of course, now the black-marketeers and the corrupt find it very difficult to store their ill-gotten money in other ways. They cannot keep it in earthen pots. That was possible when there were no currency notes and all the money one had was to be in the shape of coins – gold, silver, copper, aluminium coins, etc. Moreover, now the snooping taxmen with their Geiger counters can sniff out everything from radioactive material to currency notes. This is the age of hidden cameras. Still black money flourishes. What a miracle!

Now the wealth in the shape of shares recognised in dematerialised electronic records is the easy way out. Certain shares rose to dizzy heights during the 1999 and early 2000 boom. Only a few thousand shares of companies like Infosys, Hindustan Lever, Zee T.V., etc. were worth crores of rupees. They could be stored in a few bytes of electronic circuitry. The key to its outlet could be preserved in the shape of a smart card.

One can wonder what are the kinds ot rumours that can lead to a sudden crash? In simple forms one can say such rumours are of the same type as those which raise up the market suddenly. We know that the market is, in general, in the hands of FII's or a few Indian players who can operate most dexterously this way or that, as it suits them. Most of the investors, overwhelmingly the poorest ones, just have sheepish mentality to follow the trend blindly and such speculators are often the largest losers such that many of them go bankrupt and some of them even turn topsyturvy overnight into paupers.

Exercise 1

Understanding the passage

Put a tick mark (✓) against the true statement and a cross mark (×) against the false statement.

1. "We will pursue with policies which will enable us to realise our full potential". These words were said by the Finance Minister. ( )
2. There need not be any development in infrastructure sector if India wants to make progress. ( )
3. The stock market is often said to be the index of a country's economy. ( )
4. Most of the black money is invested in the bullion market. ( )
5. Now the wealth in the shape of shares recognised in dematerialised electronic records is the easy way out. ( )
6. The stock market is a very sensitive market. ( )
7. Rumours have no impact on the stock market. ( )
8. Sometimes, some investors burn their fingers by investing blindly in the stock market. ( )
9. It is easy to handle money in the shape of shares, etc. than to handle it in the shape of currency coins, notes, etc. ( )
10. There are certain modern devices which are used to find out the hidden currency notes, etc. ( )

Exercise 2

Comprehension

A. *Answer the following questions.*

1. Adumbrate the policies which according to Mr.Vajpayee, will enable us to realise our full potential?

____

____

2. Why the Indian Stock Market cannot be said to be the index of our country's economy?

____

____

3. Why is a speculator mostly a loser in the stock market?

____

____

4. Why should we not have blind faith in the stocks of different companies?

____

____

5. How is it easier to keep black money in the shape of shares than in the shape of coins, gold, etc.?

____

____

6. Based on the Finance Minister's explanation to the Press,

make a table of the particular years, estimated number of telephone connections required and the likely additional investment.

	Telephone connections	Outlay in dollars
2005	________________	________________
2010	________________	________________

B. ***Complete the following sentences.***

1. We will pursue with policies which ________________ ________________________________.
2. Mr. Vajpayee gave stress on ________________ ________________________________.
3. Indian Stock Market is in the hands of ________________ ________________________________.
4. A boom in the stock market causes the rise in the rates of ________________________________.
5. The stock market is often said to be ________________ ________________________________.

<u>**Exercise 3**</u>

Enrichment

A. ***Write down other words or phrases for those given below.***

1. spread : ________________
2. a sign of measure of

something : ____________

3. widespread : ____________
4. currently circulating story of uncertain truth : ____________
5. with great skill : ____________

B. ***There are some words which may take 'in-' or 'un-' to make their Antonyms e.g. credible-incredible. Tick (✓) the correct Prefix to give the Antonym of the given word.***

1. solved
   (a) un- (b) in-
2. convenient
   (a) un- (b) in-
3. consequent
   (a) un- (b) in-
4. questioned
   (a) un- (b) in-
5. constant
   (a) un- (b) in-
6. comparable
   (a) un- (b) in-
7. ready
   (a) un- (b) in-
8. real
   (a) un- (b) in-
9. conceal
   (a) un- (b) in-

Unit 35

Discipline

I PRE-READING EXERCISE

A great amount of discipline is required for the successful functioning of democracy. The word democracy contains the combining form '-cracy', which denotes a particular form of government. Now match the Columns.

1.	democracy	(a)	a government in which priests rule in the name of God
2.	autocracy	(b)	a system of government in which the priests are the rulers
3.	theocracy	(c)	a system of government by one person with absolute power
4.	bureaucracy	(d)	a government formed by the people
5.	hiercracy	(e)	a system of government in which males are dominant
6.	androcracy	(f)	a system of government in which state officials have the main power
7.	adhocracy	(g)	replacement of rigid bureaucracy with the more flexible management
8.	mobocracy	(h)	a state in which disordered crowds rule the roost

II READING COMPREHENSION

Read the passage carefully.

The word 'discipline' comes from the word 'Disciple' which means a learner. So, discipline means learning a code of conduct. Not to speak of the living beings, but non-living things also show a great deal of discipline.

The earth moves round the sun in a disciplined way. The sun rises in the east and sets in the west without failure.The earth has a gravitational force. It all happens due to the presence of great inherent discipline in these objects of nature.

Discipline creates a great sense of sociability in human beings. We take our bath daily. We brush our teeth daily. We daily comb our hair. We go to our offices or business - houses punctually. All these things keep us away from being barbarians or savages.

Discipline makes a man perfect. In certain fields like the army, agriculture and industry, discipline is of utmost importance.

If the crops are not sown and watered in a proper way and at the proper time, how can they grow? If we do not spray a pesticide in a field at the proper time and in proper order, the whole crop can be destroyed by the rodents and insects or some kind of bacteria. In that case, we, shall have to suffer a great loss.

Similarly if our defence personnel do not undergo a regular exercise, the soldiers will become lackadaisical and would not be able to prove their mettle in the hour of need.

On the same lines, if an industry does not produce its

products in the regular course of time, it will not show a satisfactory growth in the coming time. So, to do everything in the proper course of time and order is also a kind of discipline.

Discipline in a family is also of utmost importance. We learn it from our parents who try their best to make us disciplined in different walks of life. We see our father and elder brothers and sisters going to their work-places in time and returning home in time. We often notice that our parents inspire us to certain kinds of jobs and also forbid us to do certain kinds of things. Family life would be ruined if every person does whatever he likes.

Even in sports discipline has its real value. The team which has a regular exercise and the players of which obey their captain or coach, shows a good result. The players of the team who do not show much interest in discipline hardly ever win a match.

Discipline is equally important in schools and colleges. Students must learn to respect their teachers. They must learn the manners that make them civilized and sociable in society.

If a person does not care for discipline and ignores the rules of the road, he can lose some of his limbs or even his life or he can cause a grievous or even fatal injury to somebody else.

There is necessity for a great discipline in government offices, otherwise the public will have to face a great problem.

Thus discipline is the opposite of the jungle law. It is a thing of utmost importance. It also imparts to us the faculty of tolerance and makes us courageous to face many evil elements in society that try to serve their own purpose by hook or by crook.

A disciplined person accepts and praises others' superiority in any field. In case of his own superiority, he is humble and not egoistic or flamboyant. In no way is he jealous or malicious.

Exercise 1

Understanding the passage

Read the passage again. Now, put a tick mark (✓) against a true statement and a cross mark (×) against a false statement.

1. Non-living things show no deal of discipline. ( )
2. The revolving of the earth round the sun is a matter of discipline. ( )
3. Discipline makes a man cruel and selfish. ( )
4. In certain fields like army, agriculture and industry, discipline is of utmost importance. ( )
5. Watering the crops and spraying pesticides over them in time is also an act of discipline. ( )
6. If the army and other forces do not undergo a regular exercise, the soldiers will become lackadaisical. ( )
7. If industry does not give much importance to discipline and if it does not produce its products regularly, it will affect the whole of mankind. ( )

8. A family life is, usually, a disciplined life. ( )

9. The only field where there needs no discipline is the games. ( )

10. Discipline is the opposite of the jungle law. ( )

Exercise 2

Comprehension

A. *On the basis of your reading the passage, answer the following questions.*

1. Why is discipline necessary in games and sports?

____

____

2. What will happen if there is no discipline in a family?

____

____

3. How can a student observe discipline in school or college?

____

____

4. Write at least two sentences on each of the following topics.

   a. Discipline and Heavenly Bodies

____

____

b. Discipline in the Army

____

____

B. ***Give the implied meaning of the following paragraphs in one line each in the box given.***

a. Discipline creates a great sense of sociability in human beings. We take our bath daily. We brush our teeth daily. We daily comb our hair. We go to our offices or business-houses punctually. All these things keep us away from being barbarians or savages.

____

b. If the crops are not sown and watered in a proper way, how can they grow? If we do not spray a pesticide in a field at the proper time and in proper order, the whole crop can be destroyed by the rodents and insects or some kind of bacteria. In that case we shall have to suffer a great loss.

____

Exercise 3

Enrichment

A. ***One synonym for the word 'lackadaisical' is 'unenthusiastic'. Now tick the correct synonym for the word given in each set. You are to choose the word nearest in meaning to the one given.***

1. inherent
   (a) temporary (b) permanent
2. barbarian
   (a) cultured (b) uncultured
3. redoubtable
   (a) brave (b) doubtful
4. flamboyant
   (a) showy (b) simple
5. malicious
   (a) beneficial (b) harmful
6. significance
   (a) importance (b) nothingness
7. paucity
   (a) longitude (b) scarcity
8. summit
   (a) acme (b) summer

B. ***Match the words with their meanings.***

1.	lackadaisical	(a)	endurance
2.	rodents	(b)	by fair means o: foul
3.	disciple	(c)	bold
4.	tolerance	(d)	learner
5.	courageous	(e)	mammals like rats, mice, squirrels, etc.
6.	by hook or by crook	(f)	lazy

Unit 36

Friendship in Modern Terms

I PRE-READING EXERCISE

A true friend of yours will refrain from talking ill of you to others. The word 'refrain' contains the Prefix 're-' which denotes different states and actions.

Now match the Columns 'A' and 'B'. The Column 'A' contains the words which start with the Prefix 're-' (all verbs). The Column 'B' contains their meanings.

	Column A		Column B
1.	reaffirm	(a)	pay back
2.	rearm	(b)	calculate
3.	rebate	(c)	repeat the main points (of)
4.	rebuke	(d)	supply new weapons
5.	recapitulate	(e)	go back
6.	recede	(f)	express sharp disapproval
7.	reclaim	(g)	arrest again strongly
8.	reckon	(h)	obtain the return of
9.	refill	(i)	remove impurities
10.	refine	(j)	fill again

II READING COMPREHENSION

Read the passage carefully.

It is an old saying, "A friend in need is a friend indeed." But in the modern times, it is a difficult task to have a real friend. The world has got so materialized that even our good-looking friends turn false in the hour of need.

No doubt, friendship has a great value even if it is on the basis of give-and-take. In the modern society people join clubs and attend kitty parties to meet there the persons of their own tastes to expand their business.

In our neighbours we can see the people who are busy in their own work and who have no time to talk to us. In some cases, it is also found that the members of the same family have no time to talk to one another. It is because most of the people in the modern society have become slaves to all kinds of machinery like cars, computers, phones, etc. and to serve their masters, they keep themselves awfully busy in their jobs. Thus, they have to pay a heavy price and exert a lot. Do they enjoy life in the real sense when they have more friendship with dead matter than the living beings?

So busy is the nerve-straining struggle in this world of tough competition that man has to maintain friendship with his insensate masters instead of his neighbours or his real relatives. Can such a man be expected to play a game with fairness and sincerity?

The time is past when two friends played marbles together or played at cards and also tried to solve the problems of each other. In the modern society we have no time to play with our friends in the real sense. Even when we have to talk to them we make use of the phone. We meet them face to face, only when we have to do some sort of serious business deal that might bring some profit to us or when we are completely overthrown by circumstances. Thus, we have turned selfish, selfish, selfish to the core.

This system is popular with the lower as well as higher sections of society and it is prevalent there in every country. Self-interest is the hall-mark of the international society. America will continue her friendship with those countries only that buy weapons or manufactured goods from her. Russia will speak in favour of those countries that buy tanks and war aeroplanes from it. Thus most of the countries profess friendship with the countries from which they can get some benefit. The whole world trade is based on this sort of false friendship. That is why sometimes it is said, "Friendship is false and love is a farce." As a matter of fact, there are no permanent friends and foes in the international arena. The common desire for opulence and luxury which is the corner stone of the western way of life, has given a fillip to the vice of falsehood in friendship. And this fetish has invaded the Indian ethos like horde of locusts. So, let the watchword be: "Beware! Beware!"

Exercise 1

Understanding the passage

Read the passage again. Then put a tick mark (✓) against the true statement and a cross mark (×) against the false statement.

1. In the modern times we have often friends who are true ones. ( )
2. Friendship in modern times is based on the system of give-and-take. ( )

3. In every house, it is found that the members of the same family have no time to talk to one another. ( )

4. Most of the people in society are masters of machinery like cars, computers, etc. ( )

5. The time is past when two friends played marbles together. ( )

6. We meet our friends only when we are overthrown by circumstances. ( )

7. Self interest is the hall-mark of the international society. ( )

8. Even the countries like America and Russia will favour only those countries who buy some goods manufactured by them. ( )

9. The common desire for opulence and luxury which is the corner stone of the western way of life, has given a fillip to the vice of falsehood in friendship. ( )

10. So, we are enjoying a good phase of time, when the world is teeming with true friends. ( )

Exercise 2

Comprehension

A. ***Answer the following questions.***

1. Write down about the friendship in modern terms.

____

____

2. Why do people join the clubs or kitty parties?

____

____

3. To what has the modern man become a slave and why?

____

____

4. With which countries do most of the countries often profess friendship?

____

____

5. What kind of international trade is there in the world now-a-days?

____

____

6. What has accentuated the vice cf falsehood in friendship?

____

____

B. ***Complete the following sentences.***

1. Friendship even on the basis of ____________________

_________________________________ is appreciated.

2. In the modern world it is difficult to ______________

____ .

3. Even the countries like America and Russia have a stock of favourable words for those countries which ____.

4. Self-interest is the ____.

5. The modern society is a ____.

Exercise 3

Enrichment

A. ***Write down other words for those given below.***

1. terrible : ________________
2. to do a hard mental work : ________________
3. matter : ________________
4. to spread : ________________
5. depend very much upon : ________________

B. ***The antonym of the word 'opulence' is 'penury' (extreme poverty). Tick the correct Antonym for the word given below in each set.***

1. Agree
   (a) differ (b) appellate
2. Haughty
   (a) honest (b) humble
3. Diligent
   (a) indolent (b) hard-working

C. *Give the same meaning of the following passage by writing it in a different method. Do not add any idea from yourself.*

a. No doubt, friendship has a great value even if it is on the basis of give-and-take. The modern society is totally based on this method. People join clubs and attend kitty parties to meet there the people of their own tastes to expand their business.

Solved:

Undoubtedly, friendship is a valuable thing even if it is based on the give-and-take method. This is what forms the basis of modern society. People take part in clubs and kitty parties to develop their business deals.

b. In our neighbours we can see the people who are busy in their own work and who have no time to talk to us. In some cases, it is also found that the members of the same family have no time to talk to one another. It is because most of the people in the modern society have become slaves to all kinds of machinery and to serve their masters they keep themselves awfully busy in their jobs.

Solved:

____

____

____

____

____

____

____

Unit 37

School Life

I PRE-READING EXERCISE

The school students have to study many subjects, among them Maths, Chemistry, and Physics. But there are many other subjects which are not taught at school level, but have a great significance in modern times. Now match the Columns 'A' and 'B'.

Column A		Column B
1. acarology	(a)	the study of the upper atmosphere
2. aerobiology	(b)	the study or practice of travel through the air
3. aerodynamics	(c)	the study of mites and ticks
4. aeronautics	(d)	the branch of botany that deals with grasses
5. aeronomy	(e)	the study of airborne micro-organisms, etc.
6. agrology	(f)	the study of mechanical systems that function like living organisms
7. agrostology	(g)	the study of property of moving air
8. bionomics	(h)	the branch of science that deals with agriculture

II READING COMPREHENSION

Read the passage carefully.

"What is there left to tell you about my school life?", said one of the students. It is true upto certain extent of every school boy's life. His bag remains loaded with books while his mind remains loaded with a hodge-podge of different formulae of Maths, Physics, Chemistry, etc.

Almost every student gets up before the day breaks. Then he does the usual ablutions, etc. and after having breakfast, he walks out of his house with a sack-like bag, full of books and exercise-books. On the bus stop, he waits for the bus, which often arrives a few minutes late.

In the mean time, the student tosses his bag from one shoulder to the other to give rest to his tired shoulders. In this bag-oriented struggle, sometimes he gets an agonizing twist to his neck vertebrae.

Now he boards the bus with his bag in his cupped hands. "You are looking so smart, James! What a chap you are looking!" The bus gets filled with different kinds of voices.

In the school with the starting of the first period the teacher asks James to bring his exercise-book. James searches his bag twice, thrice and so on but he does not find it out. Hence no choice is left for the teacher but to punish poor James and also to order him to bring his parents with him the next morning. Nobody tries to understand why even a smart student like James is at times so absent-minded and listless.

It is only James who now realizes how he lost his exercise-book when his bag fell off his hands near the bus-stop. But who is going to believe him even if he explains every thing in all sincerity? So, he prefers to remain mum and suffers all rebukes and scoldings patiently.

Late in the evening he steps into his house, tired and bedraggled. Then his mummy cuddles and hugs her loving son and asks him, "What has happened to my lovely child"? In return, James says nothing but twists his lips and a mysterious faint smile flickers across his face. In a faltering voice he explains the day's happening. The good lady gives out a hearty laugh which seems mysterious and incredible to the nerve-shattered child who begins to sob in a suppressed voice. "Doesn't even mummy want to know me?" mumbles James to himself. This is how his agony increases till his mother kisses and hugs him again most lovingly, saying, "Take heart, my child! Nothing has gone wrong. I'll talk to your ma'am and explain everything".

Exercise 1

Understanding the Passage

Put a tick mark (✓) against the true statement and cross mark (×) against the false statement.

1. Often students have to carry a large number of books. ( )
2. A student's mind remains loaded with a confused mass of different formulae of different subjects. ( )
3. Usually a student has a small bag to carry with. ( )
4. Usually every school bus arrives in time at the stop. ( )
5. Sometimes the other students mock at the student who looks somewhat confused. ( )

6. James is listless and absent-minded because he has not had breakfast. ( )
7. Nobody tries to understand James. ( )
8. James prefers to remain mum because he is sure that nobody will believe him. ( )
9. As late in the evening James steps into his house, he looks fresh. ( )
10. James' mother cuddles her loving son. ( )

Exercise 2

Comprehension

A. ***Answer the following questions.***

1. Write down three sentences about the life of a school student as depicted in the lesson.

____

____

____

2. Why does the teacher order James' to bring his parents with him the next morning?

____

____

3. How does James' mummy treat him when he comes back from school?

____

____

4. How does James answer his mother's query?

____

____

5. Write down two sentences on the bag of a modern school student.

____

____

6. Is it only James' presumption that even his mother doesn't want to know him or do you think there is anything lacking in his mother's reception of him may be unconsciously? Answer in three sentences.

____

____

____

B. ***Complete the sentences.***

1. A student's life is a tough one because he has to carry a bag full of ___________ while his mind remains loaded ____.
2. The bag-oriented struggle sometimes proves costly to him when he gets ___________________.
3. James fishes his hands in the bag but he does not _____ ____.
4. His mummy cuddles ___________________________ ____.

5. James knows that he lost his exercise-book when ______
____.

Exercise 3

Enrichment

A. ***Write down words from the passage for the meanings given below.***

1. confusion : ______________
2. hugs : ______________
3. dishevelled : ______________
4. to get in : ______________
5. exhausted : ______________

B. ***The foreign word 'formula' has its, plural forms 'formulae and formulas'. Tick the correct plural form of the foreign words given in each set, which are mostly accepted in English Language in the modern times.***

1. radius
   (a) radii or radiuses (b) radius
2. radix
   (a) radixes (b) radices
3. peridium
   (a) peridia (b) peridiums
4. peritoneum
   (a) peritonea (b) peritoniums
5. osculum
   (a) oscula (b) osculums

<u>**Unit 38**</u>

The Value of Books

I PRE-READING EXERCISE

There are certain books which are popular world-wide.

Now match the Columns 'A' and 'B'. The Column 'A' contains the names of books. The Column 'B' contains the names of their authors.

	Column A		Column B
1.	Hamlet	(a)	Thomas Hardy
2.	Midnight's Children	(b)	Harper Lee
3.	To Kill a Mocking Bird	(c)	G.G. Marquese
4.	One Hundred Years of Solitude	(d)	Shakespeare
5.	Far From the Madding Crowd	(e)	Leo Tolestoy
6.	Gulliver's Travels	(f)	R.N. Tagore
7.	War and Peace	(g)	Jonathan Swift
8.	David Copperfield	(h)	Charles Dickens
9.	Gitanjali	(i)	Arundhati Roy
10.	The God of Small Things	(j)	Salman Rushdie

II READING COMPREHENSION

Read the passage carefully.

Knowledge has no limit as the sky has none. On the same lines, the world is limited for those who are confined to their routine work only. If you are interested in knowing what sort of ideas the modern man has, and how he differs from his ancestors, you will have to go to books for help.

There are certain things and facts that can be learnt from books only, as they were written long long ago. Through books one can judge what sort of struggle has been done by man to overcome the obstacles coming in his way to progress. Our modern civilization is not the outcome of struggle done in a single day, nor is it the result of a single man's efforts. It is the result of a bitter struggle done by the whole of mankind since man appeared on this planet and this struggle is still on, forever, never to come to an end.

Books also tell us about the progress of mind in the human race. In the beginning man feared the flashing of lightning and thundering of clouds. He was a barbarian who did not know how to respect others' ideas and emotions.

Books are not just bound pages of paper only. They contain every idea and emotion of man that he has been provided with by nature. We have some immortal books like The Mahabharata, the Ramayana, the Bible, the Koran, the Guru Granth Sahib, etc. which inspire us and show us the right path to be perfect human beings so as to make this earth a heaven.

We have books written by the most experienced minds in a state of great agony and distress such are The Scarlet Letter, Pilgrim's Progress, Paradise Lost, etc. Some books are highly tragic, for example, Shakespeare's tragedies like

Hamlet, Othello, Macbeth and King Lear. We also have books written in a cheerful and jubilant mood. Don Quixote is an example of such a kind. Another example is 'Three Men in a Boat". Then there are Shakespeare's comedies like Winter's Tale, Twelfth Night, The Merchant of Venice, As You Like It, Midsummer Night's Dream, etc. Besides books of literature and history, we have books on different topics of science. We can see even the life history of a cellular organism through zoology books. From books on botany we can get knowledge about the life history of plants.

Books written on political science tell us about the formation and elements of state and working of different kinds of government. We have books of economics, psychology, etc. which give us knowledge about their own fields.

To know the chemical and physical structure of a product, we have books of chemistry and physics respectively. Similarly, we have books on sports, art, music, dance, astrology, astronomy, geography, etc.

Similarly, we have so many other books. Through books man can know not only about this universe, but also a lot about himself. It is said that the computer is likely to end the hegemony, if not the existence, of books, but that only future will tell. The Internet is already there, but it cannot be said with certainty if it is going to diminish the utility of books.

<u>**Exercise 1**</u>

Understanding the Passage

Put a tick mark (✓) against the true statement and a cross mark (×) against the false statement.

1. Knowledge has no limit. ( )

2. To find the difference between the modern man and his ancestors, one needs the help of books. ( )

3. Books do not put light on the subject of development of man's mind. ( )

4. Right from the beginning man was a civilized creature. ( )

5. The emotions and ideas in the human beings are the gifts provided by nature. ( )

6. The holy books like the Mahabharta, the Ramayana, the Bible, the Koran, the Guru Granth Sahib, are immortal books. ( )

7. There is no such book as has ever been written in a cheerful and jubilant mood. ( )

8. Through books on zoology, one can have the knowledge about the formation of cells etc. ( )

9. Through books written on politics, one can have the idea of different kinds of games. ( )

10. Books are the store-house of knowledge. ( )

<u>Exercise 2</u>

Comprehension

A. ***Answer the following questions.***

1. What idea of the early man do you get from the passage?

____

____

____

2. Write three sentences on "Man and Civilization".

____

____

____

3. We must read books. Write down three points in favour of this proposition.

____

____

____

4. How has our modern civilization come into existence?

____

____

5. 'Books' are not just bound pages of paper only. Using your own imagination elaborate the idea.

____

____

____

6. Write down names of four immortal books.

(a) ________________ (b) ________________

(c) ________________ (d) ________________

B. *Complete the following sentences.*

1. In the beginning, man was a barbarian and he ________

____ .

2. It is the result of a bitter struggle done by ____.

3. We have books written by most experienced minds in a state of ______________________________.

4. Books also tell us about the progress ____.

5. Books contain every idea and ____.

Exercise 3

Enrichment

Match the following words with their meanings.

1.	barbarians	a)	persons, more remote than grandparents from whom one is descended
2.	agony	b)	hard
3.	ancestors	c)	the people not belonging to a good civilization or uncivilized people
4.	immortal	d)	feeling great happiness
5.	jubilant	e)	extreme anxiety
6.	distress	f)	mental suffering
7.	bitter	g)	that can never be destroyed

Unit 39

Hostel Life

I PRE-READING EXERCISE

Recognition is also an art which is applicable as much to words as to men. A sincere and inquisitive student can more easily learn the art of penetrating into the meanings of words than an indifferent or a supercilious one. Here are some common words. You are to circle the word with different meaning in each set.

1.	flamboyant	:	attractive	:	epulsive
2.	disintegrate	:	unite	:	integrate
3.	adore	:	respect	:	isrespect
4.	arrest	:	adapt	:	adjust
5.	jolly	:	attractive	:	cheerful
6.	sincere	:	serious	:	genuine
7.	uncontrolled	:	disciplined	:	controlled
8.	clever	:	intelligent	:	gentle
9.	bright	:	glimmering	:	shining
10.	salubrious	:	wholesome	:	decent

II READING COMPREHENSION

Read the passage carefully.

A great majority of students live in their own houses. But there are many students who have to live in hostels because they come from distant areas to complete their education in a school, college or university.

Hostel life is a free life in certain respects. One can get up whenever one wants. One can go to bed late at night as one has not to be afraid of one's old grandpa or one's middle-aged parents who get up in the early hours of the morning to go out for a walk or to get ready for office.

The students who are serious and are not fond of gossiping or wandering with their friends, often find themselves isolated and detached in the hostel. The strict discipline of their life according to hostel rules makes them feel sad and depressed.

The students who have jolly friends or have a delinquent behaviour are mostly boisterous and also have a flamboyant mood. They enjoy life to their heart's content in hostels.

In the hostel life there is much for a student to learn that may help him on the way to success in life. One can learn how to be self-dependent. It is because one has to arrange so many things of daily use with one's own efforts. This makes a student self-confident and he also learns the manners how to talk and behave with others in society.

Hostel life is larger than family life. One can learn here how to live together with other friends of one's own in good as well as bad times. Thus one gets the lessons of mutual help and team-spirit.

Here the students of different categories—the intelligent and the dull, the poor and the rich and of different castes live together and thus they drive home the notable point that every man has the blood of the same red colour in his veins. Thereby these hostelers give a slap on the faces of those anti-social elements who want to disintegrate our nation and society in the name of caste, colour, language, region, or creed.

Hostel life teaches co-operation. Here the students dine together, sit together and enjoy themselves together in the common room. They also play indoor games like table tennis, badminton, carom, etc. together. They organise debates and also stage plays. They take part in various functions which they themselves manage. Hence they learn how to be responsible citizens of a great nation.

Exercise 1

Understanding the Passage

Put a tick mark (✓) against the true statement and a cross mark (×) against the false statement.

1. Not all the students live in the hostels. ( )
2. Hostel life is a life of misery for most of the students. ( )
3. One has always to obey his room-mates in the hostel life. ( )
4. Some students find it boring to live in hostels because they feel isolated. ( )
5. The students who have jolly friends and who like to live in a flamboyant mood, really enjoy the hostel life. ( )

6. Hostel life makes one learn the art of doing certain jobs with one's own efforts. ( )
7. Hostel life is larger than family life. ( )
8. Hostel life is a symbol of disintegration. ( )
9. In the hostels poor and weak students are not allowed to sit in the circle of rich and strong students. ( )
10. Hostel life makes a person a responsible citizen of society. ( )

Exercise 2

Comprehension

A. ***Answer the following questions.***

1. What three things can a student learn from the hostel life?

____

____

____

2. What can be the most serious drawback of a hostel life?

____

____

3. How does hostel life help in the matter of national integration? Write three sentences.

____

____

4. Which type of students often live in hostels?

5. How does hostel life help in the matter of national integration?

6. What are the pitfalls or factors against which a hosteler must guard himself/herself which can otherwise bring about his/her ruin? Write three sentences.

B.1. ***Pick out antonyms from the following two passages and write them in the space provided. (Do not try to be arbitrary in your choice)***

I. Hostel life is a free life in certain respects. One can get up whenever one wants. One can go to bed late at night as one has not to be afraid of one's old grandpa or one's middle-aged parents who get up in the early hours of the morning to go out for a walk or to get ready for office.

II. Hostel life is a slavish life in all respects. None can get up whenever one wants. None can go to bed early at night, as none has to be afraid of one's brother who is young and who sleeps in the early hours of the evening.

Word	**Antonyms**
free	slavish
____________	____________
____________	____________
____________	____________

***Note*: Please try to frame the passage II above to adjust the Antonyms or write the new ones in a different way.**

B.2. ***Pick out antonyms from the following two passages and write them in the space provided. (Do not try to be arbitrary in your choice)***

I. The students who are serious and are not fond of gossiping or wandering with their friends often find themselves isolated and detached. The strict discipline of their life according to hostel rules makes them feel sad and depressed.

II. The students who are non-serious and are not fond of studies or staying in with their enemies never find themselves in company and attached. The lenient indiscipline of their life according to hostel rules makes them feel happy and enthusiastic.

Word	**Antonyms**
____________	____________

______________ ______________

______________ ______________

> ***Note*: Please try to adjust the Antonyms or write the new ones in a different way.**

Exercise 3

Enrichment

'A flamboyant mood' is said to be a positive mood, because it implies a cheerful demeanour, and 'a sad, or an angry mood' is said to be a negative mood. Now tick the correct answer for the words related to mood as given in each set.

1. Expectant mood

   (a) positive mood (b) negative zmood

2. Sanguine mood

   (a) positive mood (b) negative mood

3. Desperate mood

   (a) positive mood (b) negative mood

4. Morose mood

   (a) positive mood (b) negative mood

5. Despondent mood

   (a) positive mood (b) negative mood

6. Sullen mood

   (a) positive mood (b) negative mood

7. Delectable mood

   (a) positive mood (b) negative mood

Unit 40

India After Independence

I PRE-READING EXERCISE

The suffix "-cracy" denotes a system of government. Alexander Pope said about three hundred years ago: "For forms of government let fools contest; whate'er is best administered is best". Please match the Columns 'A' and 'B' given below. The following words all denote some system of government. Draw lines to match them with their meanings.

Column A	Column B
1. democracy	a) government by one person
2. aristocracy	b) government by priests in the name of God
3. mobocracy	c) system of government, elected by 'the public' through election
4. hierocracy	d) a dominant class consisting of mediocre people
5. theocracy	e) government by the nobility
6. mediocracy	f) government by one person with absolute majority
7. monocracy	g) rule by the masses
8. autocracy	h) rule by priests
9. plutocracy	i) a ruling class of rich people

II READING COMPREHENSION

Read the passage carefully.

The tyranny of the British Government was over on 15th August, 1947 when India got freedom. India became a Republic on 26th January, 1950. For the first time in 1952 the general elections were held and India became the largest Sovereign Democratic Republic in the world.

Mr. J.L. Nehru was elected the first Prime Minister of India. In his long spell of Prime Ministership, one of his most memorable contributions was the installation of heavy industry in India.

Mr. Nehru showed great interest in the construction of big dams, so that not only vast areas could be irrigated and saved from floods but also sufficient power could be produced for heavy industry as well as for agriculture.

So far, India has had a number of Prime Ministers. Among them Mrs. Indira Gandhi was also a notable figure. She tried her best to make India a strong nation. She devoted much attention to defence, industry, environmental purity and space research, particularly defence. It was so because she had to fight a crucial war with Pakistan.

After the assassination of Mrs. Indira Gandhi, her son Rajiv Gandhi was elected the Prime Minister of India. This young man showed a new way to the country by bringing supercomputer in India for the first time. The supercomputer became the heralder of the Revolution of Information Technology in India which has enhanced her status in the comity of nations and is bound to bring her prosperity undreamt of in the long run.

Mr. Rajiv Gandhi also gave great importance to the defence

sector. It was during his regime that the Bofors Gun was added to the armoury of the Indian army which proved one of the decisive factors in the 1999 Kargil Conflict against Pakistan.

Mr. Atal Behari Vajpayee is also a name not to be forgotten by the Indians. Under his Prime Ministership in spite of some of India's intractable problems like over-population, illiteracy, poverty, unemployment, etc. he has made India an economic power to be reckoned with. Under his inspiring leadership, India has gone far ahead of other countries in the matter of Information Technology. Indian companies and engineers have shown their calibre and mettle even in countries like USA, Germany, Japan, Canada, U.K., etc. India has also made great progress in the production of food-grains and milk. Now India is the largest producer of milk in the world. She is also the largest producer of fruits and second largest producer of vegetables in the world. But the cankers of corruption and communalism are still eating into the vitals of India. Let us try to eradicate them to make India a great and strong nation.

Exercise 1

Understanding the Passage

Put a tick mark (✓) against the true statement and a cross mark (×) against the false statement.

1. India got freedom on 15th August, 1947. ( )
2. Mrs. Indira Gandhi gave the maximum importance to the installation of heavy industry. ( )
3. Mr. J.L. Nehru gave the maximum importance to the Information Technology. ( )

4. After the assassination of Mrs. Indira Gandhi, her son Rajiv Gandhi was elected the Prime Minister of India. ( )

5. Mr. Rajiv Gandhi gave great importance to the defence sector and he introduced Bofors Gun in India. ( )

6. It was Rajiv Gandhi who brought the Supercomputer in India. ( )

7. The Bofors Gun was used by India against Pakistan in the war of 1965. ( )

8. In the regime of A.B. Vajpayee India has done a tremendous progress in the field of Information Technology. ( )

9. India has made great progress in the production of foodgrains and milk. ( )

10. India is the largest producer of milk in the world. ( )

Exercise 2

Comprehension

A. ***Answer the following questions in your own words basing your answers strictly on the reading of the passage.***

1. Which important method did Mr. Nehru adopt to make India a self-dependent country?

____

____

2. Name some fields to which Mrs. Indira Gandhi paid attention in particular.

____

____

3. Name two new things brought by Mr. Rajiv Gandhi in India. Also write a sentence each on the role of the things mentioned.

____

____

Sentences :

____

____

4. What is Atal Behari Vajpayee's main contribution to India?

____

____

5. Write a sentence each on the two "cankers" mentioned by the author.

____

____

B. ***Complete the following sentences.***

1. Mr. J.L. Nehru showed great interest in ____________

____ .

2. One of Mr. J.L. Nehru's most memorable contributions

was ______________________________________.

3. Mrs. Indira Gandhi devoted much attention to ________ ______________________________________.

4. Rajiv Gandhi became the Prime Minister of India after______________________________________.

5. Mr. Vajpayee is also a name not to be __________ ______________________________________.

Exercise 3

Enrichment

A. ***Give the opposite meanings of the following words by applying 'dis-' or 'mis-'.***

1. agreement : ______________
2. management : ______________
3. honest : ______________
4. place : ______________
5. locate : ______________

B. ***Some words take '-ie', after the letter 'c' e.g. financier and some words take '-ei' after 'c', e.g. 'deceive'. Now fill in the following blanks with '-ie' or '-ei'.***

1. conc — — ve	2. rec — — ve
3. omnisc — — nt	4. perc — — ve
5. anc — — nt	6. suffic — — nt
7. conc — — t	8. effic — — nt

NOTE : *In general when there is sound of 'sh', use '-ie' after 'c'.*

Unit 41

Adult Education in India

I PRE-READING EXERCISE

The word 'illiterate' stands for a person who is uneducated.

Now tick the correct word for the meanings given in each set.

1. the sharp cry of a fox

   (a) bark (b) roar

2. a large group of people or things of a particular kind

   (a) brewery (b) bevy

3. a whirring sound

   (a) burr (b) thud

4. a shrill whistle or shout of disapproval

   (a) catcall (b) dogcall

5. a positively charged ion

   (a) cation (b) anion

6. precious stone with a yellow chatoyant lustre

   (a) cat's ear (b) cat's eye

7. a person who sells cheese, butter, etc.

   (a) cheese head (b) cheese monger

8. the name of a Spanish wine

   (a) Sherry (b) Cherry

II READING COMPREHENSION

Read the passage carefully.

India has a very poor rate of literacy, much lower than that of countries like Korea, China and even Thailand. Due to this India has to face a number of problems like over-population, poverty, unemployment, etc. It is found that in the recent times, the people of this country have become more aware of these problems. Hence even the poorest are taking interest in getting their little ones educated.

But there are a large number of old people here who are totally uneducated. Being illiterate, they are unable to understand their rights and responsibilities towards their country. For them the government has planned the system of Adult Education in villages through certain systems like T.V. serials, documentary films and regular classes.

Adult Education does not mean full and detailed education. It mainly comprises knowledge of three R's. Three R's include reading, writing and arithmetic. It means only fundamental and basic knowledge which can make them aware of their basic rights and responsibilities towards their own families and also towards their nation.

Certainly going to an Adult Education Centre is a better way of getting rid of boredom than pursuit of idle hobbies like playing at cards.

Being illiterate, the elders do not know the full value of education. Most of them belong to the labour class and they want to see their little ones take up the same trade as theirs. Thus, they become instrumental in increasing the population rapidly. But they are unaware of the fact that a class one officer gets a monthly salary which may be equal to the income of their whole family for many months, may be a year even. But to be an officer one needs to be an educated one. If the old ones are educated, they can understand the value of studies and then they can try to see that their young ones take up good jobs by devoting their time to books.

Another benefit of the adult education is that when these illiterate people are educated, they will no longer be cheated by the crafty traders. They will also be able to think about jobs which can fetch them more wages.

It is not so easy a task to make a fool of an educated person. So, during the elections we can form a good government that can lead our country on the path of progress. It can happen only when our elders are educated. Only then they can know about the true value of their vote.

It is high time the government start a network of adult education centres all over the country. The teachers should be specially trained for the purpose. Students can also play a pivotal role in the project, especially during their vacation.

Exercise 1

Understanding the passage

Put a tick mark (✓) against the true statement and a cross mark (×) against the false statement.

1. Illiteracy is the root cause of population problem in India. ( )
2. A wave of awareness is there even in the lower strata of society in India. ( )

3. The illiterate are quite aware of their rights and duties. ( )

4. To attend adult education classes can be the right way for the old people to get rid of boredom. ( )

5. The old people particularly those belonging to the labour class want to see their children take up the same trade as theirs. ( )

6. It is easy for the traders to cheat an illiterate person. ( )

7. A good government can be formed in a country where the common people are illiterate. ( )

8. Adult Education is an appreciable step taken by the Indian Government. ( )

9. No specially trained teachers are needed to make he old people educated. ( )

10. An illiterate person is unable to know the real value of his vote. ( )

11. Students have no role to play in the matter of adult education. ( )

Exercise 2

Comprehension

A. ***Answer the following questions. Your answers must be based strictly on your reading of the passage unless directed otherwise.***

1. What is the main thing which the uneducated people

can't understand?

2. What steps has the government taken to make the old people educated?

3. Write down the important benefits of being educated.

4. What steps has the author suggested towards the end of the passage to speed up the project of making the old people educated?

5. Using your own imagination, write three sentences on "An Educated Nation, A Vibrant Nation."

B. ***From each of the following sentences select the word that is the closest in meaning to the underlined word. Write the answer in the box.***

1. Adult Education Centre is a better way of getting rid of

boredom than the persuit of idle hobbies.

a) foolish b) lazy
c) of great value d) none of these

2. The uneducated people want to see their little ones take up the same trade as theirs.

a) to eat b) to handle
c) to join d) none of these

3. An educated person cannot be cheated by a crafty trader.

a) cunning b) angry
c) intelligent d) none of these

4. It is not so easy a task to make a fool of an educated person.

a) matter b) talk
c) game d) none of these

5. Uneducated people are unaware that a class one officer gets a monthly salary which is equal to the income of their whole family for many months, may be a year.

a) indolent b) having no knowledge of
c) foolish d) none of these

Exercise 3

Enrichment

A. ***Give antonyms of the following words by adding Prefix 'un-' or 'ir-'.***

1. educated : ____________________
2. responsible : ____________________

3. adventurous : ____________

4. ambitious : ____________

5. reverent : ____________

B. ***'Get rid of' is a phrase. The word 'of' is frequently used in many phrases and idioms.***

Now match the Columns containing the phrases and idioms, where the word 'of' is present in each.

1. balance of power	(a) suffer the consequences of
2. fool of the first water	(b) persons of the same taste
3. a ball of fire	(c) a painful new experience
4. baptism of fire	(d) strongly resemble in a way that suggests influence
5. bear the burden of	(e) a situation in which all or some states of the world have equal power
6. bear the stamp of	(f) indulge in self-praise
7. chips of the same block	(g) a gross fool
8. boast of	(h) a person who is full of enthusiasm and energy

Unit 42

The Contemporary Indian Politics

I PRE-READING EXERCISE ,

To a really honest and conscientious man, the modern world may be a nauseating stable. Especially, the contemporary Indian politics presents a thoroughly dirty and depressing scenario. There are several negative words which express straitened circumstances in human life. Please match the Columns given below.

1.	depression	a)	an act of dying with hunger
2.	exhaustion	b)	in a state of wanting rest
3.	starvation	c)	mental efforts
4.	famine	d)	extreme tiredness
5.	restlessness	e)	severe despondency and dejection
6.	exertion	f)	scarcity of food
7.	tiredness	g)	a state of extreme physical or mental fatigue
8.	fatigue	h)	anxiety
9.	frustration	i)	not in a state of physical or emotional rest
10.	angst	j)	the state of being disappointed

II READING COMPREHENSION

Read the passage carefully.

When man awakes, all atrocious practices die. But is it because of lack of awareness among the Indian masses that the Indian politics has now reached its nadir point.

So many small parties have been formed where no one party can ever form its own government with absolute majority at the centre. Hence these the so-called servants of the nation can do whatever wrong or evil they like for self-interest and since no single party can be blamed for the malaise, all go scot-free.

Most of the politicians are perhaps billionaires. How have they attained such financial heights when the common man is groaning under the weight of abject poverty? Is it not magical? No doubt, most of them are chips of the same block. With their sweet and oily tongue, they make fool of the public and win the faith of the common man.

There should be capital punishment for the corrupt and all their property should be confiscated. But such laws will never be passed because a good number of people in the opposition are equally corrupt and even they will never press the ruling party to pass such laws.

Most influential persons, who are quite close to the politicians or bureaucrats get loans from the banks. They never pay them back. They cleverly show some sort of losses in their accounts and thus keep that loan money with themselves and in this way they get rich in a short period.

In this tight atmosphere, when the government has decreased the interest rates on bank and post office deposits, the men who get most affected are the common men particularly those who have to depend only on this interest for their living, the retired ones, the widows and such others. The Government tries to convince the people by mentioning that interest rates in the developed countries are very low. But it never tries to realize that in those countries there are so many social security measures and facilities called "Social Safety Valves", which are given to the common people, like old age pension, unemployment allowance, etc. But what is the position of an old man or an unemployed young man in India? The state governments have not money enough even to pay salaries to their employees, not to speak of pensions to pensioners.

If anybody goes to the court one can hardly expect to get justice promptly in view of lengthy judicial procedure and loopholes which the high and mighty can manage. One may say, "After all, the government has to be run". And how does the government run? A minister is going to Delhi by air to attend an important meeting. The wife of a minister is going abroad for a medical check-up.

When a common man sees himself in the grip of tentacles of inflation, corruption, decreasing bank interests, etc., he feels like bringing a turmoil in a nation like India or wants himself to be the part of the section of society that knows every trick, and that for its survival. Those who have a pure and honest soul will die in a state of depression or in the long run from exhaustion or starvation in such an atmosphere as we have in our country. The rising graph of suicides, murders, dacoities, drug-taking and other crimes and vices needs to be studied and scrutinized with much greater attention and purposefulness than ever before. But who will bell the cat to solve the man-made problems of the common man? One may ask: "When will man awake in India?"

Exercise 1

Understanding the passage

Put a tick mark (✓) against the true statement and a cross mark (×) against the false statement.

1. India is facing a situation where no one party can ever form its own government with absolute majority at the centre. ( )
2. Taking advantage of this situation, the politicians are doing whatever they like. ( )
3. It appears strict laws will be passed in India in the near future. ( )
4. The easy way to get rich in India is to show losses in one's accounts and thus keep the bank loan money with oneself. ( )
5. With the policies like the decreased interest rates on bank and post office deposits, the persons who get most affected are big businessmen. ( )
6. The state governments in India are becoming bankrupt due to misuse of funds. ( )
7. The judicial system in India is lengthy, cumbersome and full of loopholes. ( )
8. The Central Ministers do not misuse funds. ( )
9. Those who have a pure and honest soul will die in a state of depression or fromexhaustion or starvation, in the long run if the situation is not handled with great deal of honesty and alacrity. ( )
10. The rise in crime graph is the result of

increasing population only. ( )

Exercise 2

Comprehension

A. *Answer the following questions.*

1. Write down the three sentences of your own "The Contemporary Indian Politics."

____

____

____

2. How have the retired personnel been hit in the name of financial reforms?

____

____

3. How do the influential people defraud the nation of money by securing bank loans?

____

____

4. What is likely to be the fate of the honest man in India?

____

____

5. Why do not the politicians in opposition press the ruling party to pass capital punishment and confiscation of property of the corrupt?

____

____

6. What is the adverse effect of corruption and inflation on society?

____

____

B. ***Underline thePrincipal Clause in each of the following sentences.***

1. With their sweet and oily tongue they make fool of the public and win the faith of the common man.
2. When man awakes, all atrocious practices die.
3. Most of influential persons, who are quite close to the politicians get loans from the banks.
4. Those who have a pure and honest soul will die in a state of depression.
5. The men who get most affected are the common men.

Exercise 3

Enrichment

A. ***Remove 'ing' from the following words by showing the word + ing separately.***

1.	declining	=	decline	+	ing
2.	dancing	=	________	+	________
3.	wording	=	________	+	________
4.	having	=	________	+	________

5. getting = ________ + ________

6. ploughing = ________ + ________

B. *'Match the Columns', containing persons holding different positions in the world.*

1. minister	(a)	a person who acts on behalf of another
2. prophet	(b)	a female administrator of an estate
3. abbess	(c)	a person who practises allopathy
4. administratrix	(d)	a person who puts a case on someone else's behalf
5. advocate	(e)	a person who urges others to rebel or protest
6. agent	(f)	a woman who is the head of an abbey of nuns
7. agitator	(g)	a person regarded as the proclaimer of the will of God
8. allopath	(h)	the person at the head of a Department of state

Unit 43

An Ideal Citizen

I PRE-READING EXERCISE

There are several words in English which denote more than two qualities or actions or activities, though often we seldom bother to have a peep into this hilarious phenomenon.

So, please, match the Columns 'A' and ' B'. The Column 'A' contains the adjectives, each of which shows more than one quality. The Column 'B' contains the meanings of the adjectives in Column 'A'.

	Column A		**Column B**
1.	glossy	(a)	(of a writing) lengthy and uninteresting or tedious
2.	glisten	(b)	shine faintly in a wavering manner
3.	glimmer	(c)	kind and pleasant
4.	gory	(d)	shiny and smooth
5.	gracious	(e)	(of a person or process) diligent and extremely attentive to details
6.	prolix	(f)	(to be wet or greasy and) to shine
7.	scrupulous	(g)	showing violence and bloodshed
8.	vivacious	(h)	attractive and animated

II READING COMPREHENSION

Read the passage carefully.

The meaning of words 'Ideal Citizen' has been changed in the modern society. If you are quite smart and through your handsome figure, you are able to attract attention of a lot of people in society, it does not mean that you are certainly an ideal citizen. All the same it does not mean that such a man cannot be an ideal citizen.

In the modern context, if you remain mum on all the occasions and do not raise your voice against injustice you are not an ideal citizen.

An ideal citizen need not put on very simple clothes. It is also not a point that he must be an old man who may try to express himself as a bit more experienced than others. An ideal citizen can be a person with tight jeans and there can be a colourful T-shirt on his body that would make him look like a buffoon.

What is special about an ideal citizen is that he donates wholeheartedly when the money is needed by his country as it happened during the Kargil conflict. He also donates liberally during a national crisis like the Orissa cyclone, Gujarat drought, or Gujarat earthquake. In fact, he is ready to make any sacrifice for his country including the supreme sacrifice of his life. He helps the government in its pursuit of constructive policies.

Another important thing about him is that as he is a true and honest tax payer. But he also definitely asks the government to tell him where the money paid by him as income tax is being spent by it.

An ideal citizen never takes part in the agitations arranged by the political leaders for their self-interest. He comes out with full might and wisdom against the bad elements during the election hours when they try to purchase votes from the poor illiterate voters of the country. He himself can never be purchased and he enlightens others to elect only the deserving candidates.

An ideal citizen never indulges in any mal-practices like corruption, fraud, violation of laws, etc. He knows that such kind of things can cause a great damage to his country which he loves even more than his life.

He never sells anything in the black market nor does he ever purchase such items. Rather he tries to expose such kinds of people who indulge in such sort of illegal activities.

An ideal citizen never wastes diesel or petrol because he keeps no vehicle and goes everywhere on a bicycle or by bus or train. He knows that his own country is passing through rough weather and even a drop of oil is precious for the country. He also has a civic sense and he does not waste such precious things as water, electricity, gas, etc.

An ideal citizen never throws garbage or waste matter in the middle of the road or street. He keeps such things in the corner of his house and shows them match-light to burn them. It is because he is a health cautious person who knows that garbage is a magnet for the mosquitoes and flies which may spread a number of diseases. Throwing of garbage in the street means playing with one's own life and lives of one's neighbours. But he loves his neighbours and would not like to do anything wrong to them.

An ideal citizen tries to make the people, particularly those of rural areas conscious of problems like over-population, illiteracy, unemployment, child labour, etc. He also tries his best to uplift the life standard and health of women and children in particular. For that he has sometimes to quote volumes about the sacrifices of women like Lakshmi Bai, Sita, Mother Teresa, etc. Needless to say, an ideal citizen is an educated person who loves books and exploits of brave men and women.

If you have all such qualities in you, then you are an ideal citizen. Even otherwise you should not lose heart. You can develop these and similar qualities in you. Remember that even a poor person can be an ideal citizen. To be an ideal citizen needs no money. These are will, consciousness and inclination of mind which are essential to make one an ideal citizen. And last but not least, an ideal citizen tries his utmost to remove social inequalities and economic disparities from the world.

Exercise 1

Understanding the passage

Put a tick mark (✓) against the true statement and a cross mark (×) against the false statement.

1. One who looks smart is certainly an ideal citizen in the modern society. ( )
2. It is not necessary for an ideal citizen to raise voice against the government for its wrong policies. ( )
3. Even a person having buffoon type personality can be an ideal citizen. ( )
4. An ideal citizen will always be a true and honest tax payer. ( )

5. An ideal citizen is not willing to ask the government where the money paid by him as income tax is being spent by it. ( )

6. An ideal citizen only rarely indulges in malpractices like corruption, fraud, etc. ( )

7. An ideal citizen tries to make the people of rural areas educated about the problems like over-population, unemployment, etc. ( )

8. An ideal citizen is so busy that he has no time to deal with the social problems. ( )

9. An ideal citizen only minds his own business and he does not care if his surroundings are clean or unclean. ( )

10. A poor person can never be an ideal citizen. ( )

11. An ideal citizen has nothing to do with social or economic inequalities. ( )

Exercise 2

Comprehension

A. ***Answer the following questions.***

1. Write two sentences about the possible peculiar or untraditional traits of a modern ideal citizen.

   (a) about physical features

   ____

   (b) about dress

   ____

2. How an ideal citizen can be a boon to the society and the nation?

____

____

3. Why does an ideal citizen go everywhere on foot or bicycle or by bus or train?

____

____

4. Write three sentences of your own on "An Ideal Citizen."

____

____

____

5. Using your own imagination, explain how social and economic disparities can be removed from the world, especially from India.

____

____

____

B. ***Complete the following sentences.***

1. In the modern context, if, you remain mum on all the occasions and ______________________________.

2. An ideal citizen never indulges in the practices of ______________________________.

3. An important thing about an ideal citizen is that he is a true ______________________________.

4. Throwing of garbage in the street means ____________ ______________________________.

Exercise 3

Enrichment

A. ***Write down the meanings of the following words.***

1.	(a)	ideal	:	____________
	(b)	idle	:	____________
	(c)	idol	:	____________
2.	(a)	conflict	:	____________
	(b)	fight	:	____________
	(c)	war	:	____________
3.	(a)	drought	:	____________
	(b)	draught	:	____________
	(c)	draughts	:	____________

B. ***Tick the correct answer.***

1. Buffoon
   (a) carton (b) cartoon
2. Indolent
   (a) ideal (b) idle
3. To wear
   (a) to put on (b) to put by

Unit 44

Subhash Chandra Bose

I PRE-READING EXERCISE

In this unit we are going to use the adjective 'revolutionary' which ends in the letter, 'y'. There are many more adjectives which end in the letter 'y'.

Now match the Columns 'A' and 'B'. The Column 'A' contains the adjectives ending in 'y' while the Column 'B' contains their meanings.

	Column A		Column B
1.	balmy	(a)	(mathematics) using only 0 and 1 as a system of numbers
2.	bandy	(b)	divided into equal horizontal bars
3.	barry	(c)	full of knots
4.	benedictory	(d)	pleasant warm (weather)
5.	bimilenery	(e)	arrogant
6.	boxy	(f)	curved
7.	cheeky	(g)	relating to giving of a blessing
8.	cocky	(h)	irreverent
9.	knotty	(i)	squarish in shape
10.	binary	(j)	relating to a period of two thousand years

II READING COMPREHENSION

Read the passage carefully.

India is a land of saints and heroes. There have been in India the apostles of peace and non-violence like Mahavir, the Buddha, Guru Nanak, and Gandhi. But there also have been in India great and brave heroes and warriors like Rana Pratap, Shivaji and Guru Gobind Singh. Subhash Chandra Bose was one of such brave men. He believed that the British people could not be ousted from the Indian soil just by begging, petitioning or passive non-co-operation agitations. He believed in an armed struggle against the British Government.

Subhash Chandra Bose was born on 23rd January, 1897 in Cuttak in Orissa. The name of his father was Mr. Jankinath Bose who was a successful lawyer. His mother's name was Mrs. Prabha Vati who was a highly religious lady and was a devotee of Swami Ramakrishna Paramhansa. Like Shivaji and Gandhiji, Subhash's mother had a deep influence on him. He imbibed a religious and spiritual outlook from her. Another reason for his religious outlook of life was the influence of his teacher Parsad Madho on him. Swami Vivekananda's sermons also had a deep impact on him.

However, Subhash had the signs of a revolutionary spirit in him from the very beginning. He passed his Intermediate Examination in the first Division in 1915. However, it is now proverbially known that as a student of Presidency College, Calcutta, he slapped his teacher when the latter spoke against India and the Indian people. He was rusticated but later readmitted. He did graduation in 1919.

Subhash's father wanted him to pass the ICS examination and become a high officer. He had no intention to serve the

British Government. Yet he appeared in the ICS examination which was then held in England. He got the fourth position. He, however, refused to serve the British Government.

In 1921, he returned to India. Subhash was more impressed by the way of thinking of Sri Aurobindo and Lokmanya Tilak than of Gandhiji. Hence he did not participate in the Non-co-operation Movement.

Subhash came under the influence of C.R. Das who was trying to promote the cause of freedom movement by spreading education. He also brought out a paper. Acting upon C.R. Das's advice, Subhash did as he desired and became popular with the people of Bengal. However, he was imprisoned for six months for leading a protest march against the visit of the Prince of Wales to India.

In 1924, Subhash was sent to Mandalay jail in Burma (Myanamar) for his association with the revolutionaries. But he was set free in 1927 on health grounds. Later he made even more sacrifices which the nation can never forget. It is said that he died in 1945 in an aircrash. But his death in 1945 is still contested by many. In any case, the Indian people can never forget this brave son of India who is lovingly and reverentially called "Netaji".

Exercise 1

Understanding the Passage

Put a tick mark (✓) against the true statement and a cross mark (×) against the false statement.

1. India is a land of brave men and saints. ( )
2. Subhash Chandra Bose believed that the British people could be ousted from the Indian soil by

repeated request. ( )

3. Subhash Chandra Bose was born on 23rd January, 1897. ( )
4. The name of his father was Jankinath Bose who was a successful lawyer. ( )
5. Subhash Chandra Bose's mother was a highly religious lady. ( )
6. Subhash Chandra had the signs of a revolutionary spirit in him from the very beginning. ( )
7. Subhash's father wanted his son to pass the ICS examination and become a high officer. ( )
8. Subhash was more impressed by the way of thinking of Gandhiji than Lokmanya Tilak. ( )
9. Subhash Chandra Bose acted upon the advice of J.L. Nehru. ( )
10. In 1924, Subhash was sent to Mandalay jail in Burma (Myanamar) for his association with the revolutionaries. ( )

Exercise 2

Comprehension

A. ***Answer the following questions.***

1. Write down three sentences about the family of Subhash Chandra Bose.

____

____

2. What sort of freedom fighter was Subhash?

3. Why did Subhash refuse to become an officer?

4. What shows that Subhash had a sincere patriotic spirit in him?

5. How did Subhash become popular with the people of Bengal?

6. Write a few words on "Subhash Chandra Bose – A Revolutionary"

B. ***Complete the following sentences.***

1. Subhash's father wanted him to be an officer but ______

______.

2. Subhash did not participate in the Non-co-operative Movement because ______________________________

____ .

3. Subhash was imprisoned for six months because ______

____ .

4. Subhash was highly impressed by ________________

____ .

5. The names of a few apostles of peace are ____________

____ .

<u>**Exercise 3**</u>

Enrichment

Write down the words for the meanings given below.

1. prophet : ________________
2. uproar : ________________
3. expelled : ________________
4. meeting : ________________
5. famous : ________________

Unit 45

The Beggar Problem in India

I PRE-READING EXERCISE

There are many qualities, any of which a man may have, e.g. a beggar may be 'bold'.

Now match the Columns 'A' and 'B'. The Column 'A' contains the names of qualities and the Column 'B' contains a detail of them.

Column A		**Column B**
1. covetous	(a)	sensitive
2. coy	(b)	having good sense
3. craven	(c)	delightful
4. boisterous	(d)	having or showing a great desire to possess something that belongs to someone else.
5. bumptious	(e)	shy or modest
6. foxy	(f)	cowardly
7. delicate	(g)	self-assertive
8. delectable	(h)	cunning or crafty, i.e. having the skill of achieving one's ends by deceit or evasion
9. judicious	i)	noisy and cheerful

II READING COMPREHENSION

Read the passage carefully.

Being a densely populated country full of illiterate and semi-literate people, India is one of the poorest countries in the world. She can probably boast of having the largest begging force in the world and it is a challenge to the whole society, even to the whole of mankind.

The government is trying its best to give incentives and subsidies for the installation of different industries to meet this problem of begging the roots of which lie in the problem of unemployment and generous nature of average Indians.

The crafty industrialists know the problem of the government and they also know the loopholes in the laws. Hence they are enjoying all the incentives like loans and subsidies declared by the government for industry even without installing any industrial plant. Thus they are playing with the dreams of the people, duping the government and trampling on the rights of the beggars who cannot be given employment and rehabilitated for want of funds. It happened particularly during the nineties when a large number of industrialists cornered money through public issues and flew away overnight without leaving their foot-prints behind.

The most hated section of the society, called beggars is a horde of parasites. A beggar is a burden on society. Nothing good can be expected of him. He eats and drinks even without doing anything for his country. He marries as other people do. Thus he multiplies the population of the country at a tremendous rate and gives more and more beggars to India.

One can see these beggars in groups or pairs at railway stations, at bus stops, and near religious places. It is because begging is an easy occupation for them. Moreover, our religion teaches us to give alms to the needy and the poor. These beggars play with the sentiments of religious persons and get a part of their earnings without doing anything good to them or to the country.

Mostly these beggars live in slums. Those who do not have their own accommodation spend their lives on the footpaths, at railway stations or bus stands. They live in very unhealthy and unhygienic environment. They seldom bathe or wash their clothes.

Many of them are past-masters in the art of begging. They pretend to be blind or dumb or deaf, etc. Thus they stir our emotions and win the sympathy of the common people.

Some of them have an understanding with anti-social elements. Such beggars do much harm to society by abducting little children or by smuggling narcotics. Some of them even do espionage against their own country.

They are downright traitors and must be dealt with as such.

The Government should take strict result - oriented steps to get this section of society employed in some useful occupation. More industrial units should be installed and thus more employment avenues should be opened. Not only begging but also giving alms to beggars should be prohibited by law.

In the western countries the problem of begging is not so acute as it is in India. It is because these countries have good laws and a more effective system of justice. The people in these countries are largely educated. They always make efforts to see themselves at the higher places in society. But in a country like India, the poor and illiterate people enjoy wallowing in the ditches of poverty and are unaware of the real personality of a person. They have no idea of the value of self-respect. No wonder that such people should take pride even in begging. And the irony is that most of the Indians, even if they do not address one another with due respect, have all the regards for a beggar, especially if he appears in ochre or some other peculiar dress and if he can sing or utter, in however revulsive voice, some well-crammed hymns, couplets or platitudes.

Exercise 1

Understanding the Passage

Put a tick mark (✓) against the true statement and a cross mark (×) against the false statement.

1. Begging is not a serious problem in India. ( )
2. The industrial growth has a great impact on the financial condition of a country. ( )
3. There is no stability in the Indian industrial sector. ( )
4. The crafty businessmen are enjoying all incentives and loans and subsidies declared by the government even without installing any industrial plant. ( )
5. A beggar is, in fact, a parasite. ( )
6. Beggars in India usually can be seen near the graveyards, wine shops, etc. ( )

7. Beggars play with the sentiments of religious persons and get a part of their earnings even without doing any work. ( )

8. One should remain careful about these beggars because some of them have their connections with the anti-social elements. ( )

9. In the poor countries like India the poor and illiterate people are quite aware of the real personality of a person. ( )

10. Most of the Indians have a great respect for the beggars who wear ochre and sing hymns. ( )

Exercise 2

Comprehension

A. ***Answer the following questions.***

1. What are the main causes of increase in the number of beggars in India?

____

____

2. How can the problem of begging be solved in India?

____

____

3. What harms are done to society by these beggars? Write two sentences.

____

____

4. What tricks do the beggars play to stir our emotions?

____

____

5. Suggest some amendment in the law against begging. You may use your own imagination, if necessary.

____

____

6. On the basis of your reading the passage and on your own observation, describe the physical features of an Indian beggar.

____

____

____

B. ***On the basis of your reading the passage, write down the meanings of the following lines.***

1. Stir our emotions ______________________________
2. Enjoy wallowing in the ditches of poverty __________

   ____.
3. They are playing with the sentiments of religious person

   ____.
4. A number of industrialists cornered money through public issues and flew away overnight without leaving their foot-prints behind ____________________

   ____.

5. Many of them are past-masters in the art of begging

____.

Exercise 3

Enrichment

There are some words which take 'un' when they are used as Adjectives but they take 'in' when are used as Nouns.

Now tick (✓) the correct word in each set.

1. ability
   (a) inability (b) unability
2. able
   (a) inable (b) unable
3. civil
   (a) incivil (b) uncivil
4. civility
   (a) incivility (b) uncivility
5. just
   (a) injust (b) unjust
6. justice
   (a) injustice (b) unjustice
7. equal
   (a) inequal (b) unequal
8. equality
   (a) inequality (b) unequality

Unit 46

The Two Sides of Science

I PRE-READING EXERCISE

The art of writing is a part and parcel of modern life. It manifests itself in several shapes, chiefly books. Books are now available on any and every subject. But the modern age being the age of science, scientific books have their own significance. Given below are some words which are mainly concerned with study, science or writing in one way or the other. Please match the Columns.

1.	autobiography	a)	handwriting, different from typography
2.	biography	b)	study pertaining to population
3.	calligraphy	c)	bad handwriting
4.	cryptography	d)	decorative handwriting
5.	cacography	e)	an account of a person's life written by that person
6.	chirography	f)	a list of the books referred to in a scholarly work
7.	bibliography	g)	the art of solving codes
8.	demography	h)	an account of someone's life written by someone else

II READING COMPREHENSION

Read the passage carefully.

Since man's appearance on earth he has remained an important part of nature. In the beginning the things lacked their names and needed symbols to be described. This is how strange sounds and hieroglyphic languages developed.

On the other hand, man lived in dense jungles like other animals. He feared the flashing of lightning and thundering of clouds. But day after day man's brain got filled with scientific ideas mainly through observation and experience. By and by he got success in discovering and inventing many things which made his life more comfortable. Now he has understood the mystery of nature to some extent, if not fully. All this did not happen overnight. It took thousands of years.

Man has discovered and invented many important things in every walk of life. The discovery of electricity has made his life comfortable as now he uses so many electric gadgets for this purpose.

Now man is out of barbarism and savagery except for a few pockets on the face of the earth. He has developed a society which is comparatively stable, peaceful and durable.

The rapacious mind of man still never stopped and the flame of desire to conquer nature always remair ed burning in his mind. Thus man invented aeroplanes to move about to different countries across the world. When the aeroplane was invented, it was totally out of man's mind that, this machine could one day be used in wars and could prove to be one of the most useful as well as dangerous things for mankind.

There came the steam engine, diesel engines and now we can see electric engines running on the railway tracks. These aeroplanes and electric trains are able to run at a great speed and save man's precious time.

Now we have telephones, fax, mobile phones, cordless phones, etc. to talk to our friends or relatives who are living in different parts of the world. We have watches to get ready for our offices in time.

There has been a great progress in the agricultural field. Biotechnology is quite a new science.

In the field of medicine man has made a tremendous progress by discovering so many new organisms that are harmful to man and he has also found the ways to get rid of them. Now-a-days, T.B., leprosy and even cancer to some extent are curable. Any kind of disease or mysterious problem to the human body can be detected with the help of different instruments invented by man.

In the field of space and information technology man has done a great job. With the help of rockets man has put his foot on the land of the moon. With the help of satellites man is able to see the things happening even at the deepest layer of the earth and the bottom of the sea. The computer has made man's work faster and easier. Even a biocomputer may be invented in course of time.

However, being a social animal, man fears his own brethren the most. To tackle the problem, man has invented hydrogen bombs, atom bombs, neutron bombs, missiles, etc. All this destructive material has come into being due to the discovery of the atom which has thus proved both a blessing and a curse. Now man is living under great tension. He is quite aware that all this destructive material can annihilate the whole of mankind. In the World War II, the atom bombs that were dropped on Japan's two important cities, showed their destructive force and the foolishness of the human mind thus came on the surface.

At present, one can say man has done a lot. He can do much more. Perhaps he can do anything except that he cannot overcome his fear - fear from himself and his brethren. Should we call it a cruel joke played by man on man himself or an irony of fate when man is still not certain whether he will be able to continue his existence on this planet and, if so, for how long? Thus, man is surrounded by the dazzling sun-light of knowledge, but like a little baby, he is afraid of his own shadow. Should we call man an "adult" or "a little baby"?

Exercise 1

Understanding the passage

Put a tick mark (✓) against the true statement and a cross mark (×) against the false statement.

1. From the very beginning man had given names to the things around him. ( )
2. In the ancient times, man lived in muddy houses. ( )
3. Man in early stages feared the flash of lightning and thundering of clouds. ( )
4. With the passage of time man invented and discovered many things that proved useful to him. ( )

5. Man has a curious mind; that is why he always possesses the desire to conquer nature. ( )
6. In the field of medicine man has made a tremendous progress by discovering thec harmful organisms and he has also found the way to get rid of them. ( )
7. The invention of dangerous weapons is the result of man's efforts to overcome his own fear from his own brethren. ( )
8. The satellites do not help to see the things at the bottom of the sea. ( )
9. Man is sure that he will live forever on the surface of the earth. ( )
10. It is easy for man to overcome his fear from his brethren. ( )

<u>Exercise 2</u>

Comprehension

A. ***Answer the following questions.***

1. How has science enabled man to come out of barbarism and savagery? Write down three sentences.

____

____

____

2. What does man fear the most?

____

3. What destructive materials have been developed by the man in the recent times?

4. Write down the roles of satellites in the modern man's life. You may use your own imagination.

5. How is man still a little baby?

6. How are aeroplanes a double-edged weapon?

B. ***Use the underlined phrases in sentences of your own.***

1. Now man is <u>out of barbarism</u>.

2. The flame of fire to conquer nature always remained burning <u>in his mind</u>.

3. Man has done a great job <u>in the fields of</u> space and information technology.

4. <u>With the help of</u> satellites man is able to see the things happening even at the deepest layer of the earth.

____

5. Destructive material can finish <u>the whole of mankind</u>.

____

<u>Exercise 3</u>

Enrichment

Tick the correct option to see whether it will take 'e' or 'ee'.

1. sat – llite
   (a) e (b) ee
2. engin – r
   (a) e (b) ee
3. ej – ctor
   (a) e (b) ee
4. el – gant
   (a) e (b) ee
5. fl – ce
   (a) e (b) ee
6. fr – t
   (a) e (b) ee

<u>**Unit 47**</u>

The Value of Trees

I PRE-READING EXERCISE

Trees and plants give us different kinds of fruits and vegetables which are used for eating or in different preparations like jams, pies, cakes, pickles, etc. Now Match the Columns. The Column 'A' contains the names of some eatables and the Column 'B' contains their contents, etc.

Column A		Column B
1. grisette	(a)	an edible yam
2. grits	(b)	a plant, the young shoots of which are used as food
3. adjigo	(c)	an edible mushroom with a brown or grey cap
4. adzuki	(d)	a preserve made from oranges, etc.
5. artichoke	(e)	round red edible bean
6. asparagus	(f)	coarsely ground corn kernels
7. marmalade	(g)	herb with spicy seeds used for flavouring pickles
8. dill	(h)	name of a plant with flowering head which is used as a vegetable

II READING COMPREHENSION

Read the passage carefully.

Trees have been making sacrifices for man since the origin of the earth. In ancient times man made his shelter under the trees. He also used trees to make his wooden weapons. As the fire was discovered, man burnt the trees to make himself warm in the bitter coldness. Later tree wood was also used and is still used to make boats.

Trees not only give us fruits but they are also the base of the paper industry. They are also used to make match sticks.Different kinds of tree-wood is used to make doors, furniture and decorative material for the houses and offices.

On the other hand, trees also prevent floods. It is because the trees don't allow soil erosion.

Even at present in some areas of the world the houses are made of tree-wood. The areas in which there are frequent earthquakes, often have houses of wood.

Trees also give shelter to the wild beasts like tiger, lion, rhinoceros, etc. Otherwise, the cruelty of man will not allow them to breathe on this globe and they will remain only the creatures to be read about in illustrated books.

Trees absorb carbon from carbon dioxide in the air and release oxygen. Thus they maintain oxygen balance in air. In the absence of trees, there will be paucity of oxygen in air without which man can't live.

Trees also give shelter to the birds. On the branches of trees the birds make their nests and lay eggs and we all know, there are so many species of birds in the world which are very beneficial to man in one way or the other.

We get medicines from many plants, like acacia, cinchona, etc. We also get rubber from rubber plants, which is used by man in many ways in his daily life. Trees produce not only life-saving drugs for mankind but also coal (may be centuries after their death).

Our government has taken certain important steps to increase the area of forests so as to keep the earth green. As we know, woods are necessary to ensure the rainfall which is so important for us. Special rules and regulations have been made to save the woods across the country. Still, the process of felling down trees has been on the rise in recent times. "Vanmahotsav" is celebrated in July each year to inspire the whole nation to grow more trees to protect the environment and maintain oxygen balance in air. This process was started by Mr. K.M. Munshi, then a minister in the Union Cabinet. The government is trying to increase the green area.. Sufficient progress has been made in and around Delhi in this respect. But much needs to be done elsewhere.

Exercise 1

Understanding the passage

Put a tick mark (✓) against the true statement and a cross mark (×) against the false statement.

1. Trees have an important role in man's life. ( )
2. In ancient times weapons were made of the tree wood. ( )
3. Nowadays the tree wood is used to decorate the houses and this is the only thing that now trees provide us. (

4. Trees have no role in maintaining the balance of oxygen in the atmosphere. ( )

5. Many trees like acacia and cinchona are used to prepare medicines. ( )

6. A dead tree is of no use. ( )

7. The Indian government has taken certain necessary steps to save the trees. ( )

8. The felling of trees across the country has shown a downward trend in the recent times. ( )

9. "Vanmahotsav" is celebrated in the month of December. ( )

10. Trees provide life to man by releasing oxygen. ( )

<u>Exercise 2</u>

Comprehension

Answer the following questions.

1. What are the benefits of trees to man?

____

____

2. Why should we grow more trees?

____

____

3. How are the trees beneficial to birds? Write down two sentences.

____

____

4. What would happen to this earth if there were no tree? Give at least two arguments.

____

____

5. Make a list of the wooden furniture in your house. Write six items.

a) ____________ b) ____________

c) ____________ d) ____________

e) ____________ f) ____________

6. Suggest some ways to protect the trees.

____

____

____

B. ***Complete the following sentences.***

1. The trees prevent floods because ____________

____.

2. Our government has taken certain important ____________

____.

3. We get medicines from plants like ____________

____.

4. In the absence of trees, there will be ____________

____

5. Still, the process of felling down of trees ____________

____.

Exercise 3

Enrichment

Find out the difference between the following pairs of words by using them in sentences of your own.

1. (a) fall

   ____

   (b) fell

   ____

2. (a) roll

   ____

   (b) role

   ____

3. (a) environment

   ____

   (b) atmosphere

   ____

Unit 48

Salesmanship

I PRE-READING EXERCISE

With the predominance of the marketing faculty in the field of manufacturing trade and commerce, salesmanship has assumed great importance these days. A salesman has a direct relationship with the customer and they together arouse the display of certain common words in their own context. Please circle the word which is different in meaning from the others in each set.

1. profession	:	business	:	game
2. contented	:	dissatisfied	:	satisfied
3. attractive	:	infectious	:	repulsive
4. cynic	:	nincompoop	:	fool
5. deficiency	:	abundance	:	scarcity
6. acquainted	:	unknown	:	familiar
7. disagreed	:	convinced	:	agreed
8. untrue	:	sincere	:	genuine
9. captivate	:	repel	:	fascinate

II READING COMPREHENSION

Read the passage carefully.

The first and foremost duty of a salesman is to promote the sales of the cocnern he serves. But to do this, he must have some essential qualities which can attract and satisfy customers.

So, in an indirect way, to satisfy his customers becomes ipso facto the second important duty of a salesman.

In this respect, a salesman works as a bridge between the seller and the customer. There can be different varieties of salesmen like the counter-salesmen and the travelling salesmen. Now-a-days, there are even salesmen who go from door-to-door to sell various items. They may be called door-to-door salesmen.

In all cases, the salesmen (or sales-women or girls which is implicit in the term) must have the following qualities, inter-alia, to be successful in their profession.

A salesman must have a pleasing personality. He should show his teeth in smiles - rather than in grins. Thus he must attract customers like a magnet. It is said smiles are infectious. So, when he smiles, the customers may be expected to smile with him. But that is possible only if the customers are really satisfied.

This means that he must be able to satisfy his customers. The customers can feel satisfied if they are really convinced.

One may ask: "Convinced about what?" The simple answer is: convinced about the quality, quantity, price and guarantee of the product.

This brings us to an important point which is not concerned merely with the salesman. It is that the product must be genuine and of a good quality and the price must be genuine. There should be no effort there to fleece the customers. The customers should not be considered nincompoops or novices as some sellers or manufacturers take them for. This point certainly relates to the producer or the manufacturer. A trader must simply refuse to purchase and sell the articles of a dishonest or bogus manufacturer. If the product itself is defective in one way or the other, even the best salesman may not be able to promote it. If he feels the trader only wants to indulge in malpractices, he should simply refuse to work in such a concern or ask his master frankly to mend his ways.

A good salesman is expected to explain the qualities of a product in a simple but convincing way. He must be acquainted with the customers' psychology, particularly the psychology of women, children and old men. He must ensure that the products sold are properly and attractively packed. Finally, a salesman must be well-dressed, neat and clean and be neither reticent nor a bragging one.

Naturalness, sincerity, frankness, politeness, transparency, fluency in speech, and neatness collectively frame the key to success for a salesman.

<u>Exercise 1</u>

Understanding the passage

Put a tick mark (✓) against the true statement and a cross mark (×) against the false statement

1. A salesman must have some essential qualities to attract and satisfy customers. ( )

2. Now-a-days salesmen do not go from door-to-door to sell various items. ( )

3. When a salesman smiles, the customers may be expected not to smile with him. ( )

4. The products must be genuine and of good quality, no matter what the prices are. ( )

5. The trader must refuse to purchase and sell the articles of a bogas manufactures. ( )

6. A good salesman must be acquainted with the customers psychology. ( )

7. A salesman should not refuse to work with a trader who wants to indulge in malpractices. ( )

8. Politeness, sincerity, and fluency in speech collectively frame the key to success for a salesman. ( )

Exercise 2

Comprehension

A. ***Answer the following questions.***

1. What is the main duty of a salesman?

____

____

2. What are the qualities of a good salesman?

____

____

3. When does even the best salesman fail to promote a product?

____

____

4. Name at least three kinds of salesmen.

____

____

____

5. Can we say that a good salesman is a versatile genius?

____

____

6. Enumerate the constituents of the "collective frame" of the key to success for a salesman.

____

____

____

B. ***Complete the following sentences.***

1. A good salesman must bring to his master's notice

____.

2. A salesman should refuse to work when __________

____.

3. A salesman should keep smiling because __________

____.

4. A salesman should know in particular the psychology of ______________________________.

5. A salesman must be well-dressed, neat and clean, and be neither______________________________.

Exercise 3

Enrichment

A. ***Write down the textual words or phrases for the meanings given below.***

1. fools : ______________
2. real : ______________
3. familiar : ______________
4. loot : ______________
5. boasting : ______________

B. ***Give Antonyms of the following words.***

1. foremost : ______________
2. pleasing : ______________
3. possible : ______________
4. convinced : ______________

Unit 49

O' Sweet, Sweet Small Bird!

I PRE-READING EXERCISE

Write down the letter/s which is/are silent in each of the following words in the space provided and re-write the word again with the silent letter/s in brackets as shown hereunder:

	Word	Silent Letter	Word Re-written
1.	comb	b	com (b)
2.	adjust	__________	__________
3.	eureka	__________	__________
4.	honesty	__________	__________
5.	stalk	__________	__________
6.	deck	__________	__________
7.	condemn	__________	__________
8.	gnome	__________	__________
9.	servant	__________	__________
10.	psyche	__________	__________
11.	knob	__________	__________
12.	parliament	__________	__________
13.	single	__________	__________

II READING COMPREHENSION

Read the passage carefully.

"O Sweet, Sweet Small Bird!
What do you sing?
Will you for me
Some flowers bring?

From that distant garden
Off the canal;
I know that you can
Fly o'er the wall!

O please go and come back
In half a jiffy;
Don't shrug your shoulders
Nor grow so fluffy!"

"O Sweet, Sweet Small Child!
Don't be so huffy;
I'll go across the wild
To that garden puffy,

And bring you flowers
Pink, red and blue
And, if you so wish,
Of every hue".

"O thanks! I've to offer
A colourful bouquet
To my dear mother
On her happy birthday!"

By H.S. BHATIA

Exercise 1

Comprehension

Answer the following questions.

1. Please write in simple prose what the child wants the bird to do for him.

   ____

   ____

2. Write down the lines which suggest that the bird is hesitant in obeying the child.

   ____

   ____

   ____

   ____

3. What assurance does the bird give to the child? Write in simple prose.

   ____

   ____

4. Write down the lines which suggest that the child loves his mother dearly.

   ____

   ____

   ____

   ____

5. The poem consists of six quatrains (i.e., of six stanzas comprising four lines each). In each stanza the second line rhymes with the fourth. Please make a list of all the rhyming words.

Stanza

(1) sing	and	bring
(2) ________	and	________
(3) ________	and	________
(4) ________	and	________
(5) ________	and	________
(6) ________	and	________

Exercise 2

Give Antonyms of the following.

1. grow : ____________
2. distant : ____________
3. bring : ____________
4. sweet : ____________
5. dear : ____________